PENGUIN B{
BEYOND BOUN

Swraj Paul was born in Jalandhar in 1931. He was educated at Doaba College, the University of Punjab, and the Massachusetts Institute of Technology, USA. After some years in the family business in Calcutta, he went to England in 1966 and established the Caparo Group, a UK-based international manufacturing business.

Swraj Paul is Pro-Chancellor of Thames Valley University and is the author of a well-received biography of Indira Gandhi published in 1984. He is married to Aruna Paul, nee Vij, and they have four children. Awarded the Padma Bhushan by the Government of India in 1983, he became a member of the British House of Lords in 1996.

SWRAJ PAUL

Beyond Boundaries
A Memoir

PENGUIN BOOKS

PENGUIN BOOK

Published by the Penguin Group

Penguin Books India Pvt. Ltd, 11 Community Centre, Panchsheel Park, New Delhi 110 017, India

Penguin Group (USA) Inc., 375 Hudson Street, New York, New York 10014, USA

Penguin Group (Canada), 90 Eglinton Avenue East, Suite 700, Toronto, Ontario, M4P 2Y3, Canada (a division of Pearson Penguin Canada Inc.)

Penguin Books Ltd, 80 Strand, London WC2R 0RL, England

Penguin Ireland, 25 St Stephen's Green, Dublin 2, Ireland (a division of Penguin Books Ltd)

Penguin Group (Australia), 250 Camberwell Road, Camberwell, Victoria 3124, Australia (a division of Pearson Australia Group Pty Ltd)

Penguin Group (NZ), cnr Airborne and Rosedale Roads, Albany, Auckland 1310, New Zealand (a division of Pearson New Zealand Ltd)

Penguin Group (South Africa) (Pty) Ltd, 24 Sturdee Avenue, Rosebank, Johannesburg 2196, South Africa

Penguin Books Ltd, Registered Offices: 80 Strand, London WC2R 0RL, England

First published in Viking by Penguin Books India 1998
Published in Penguin Books 1999

Copyright © Swraj Paul 1998

Typeset in New Baskerville by SÜRYA, New Delhi
Printed at DeUnique, New Delhi-18

To

My Loving Parents
of whom I knew so little

My Caring Brothers
to whom I owe so much

My Dearest Aruna
with whom I share so much

My Beloved Ambika
for whom so little was so much

Contents

Preface

In February 1996, I celebrated my sixty-fifth birthday. This was a landmark event for me. Thirty years earlier I had come to live in Britain and during the intervening decades my life had changed in the most unusual ways. The business which I had begun with a small loan and a lot of hope is now the largest family-owned enterprise in the United Kingdom. From its origins in a small and unpretentious building in Huntingdon, some sixty miles north of London, Caparo has become a successful multinational operation with modern manufacturing facilities in five countries and over four thousand workers.

More than that, I have enjoyed an extraordinarily happy family life. Aruna and I have been married for forty-one years—itself something of an achievement in these restless days. We have been blessed with four loving children and six grandchildren. There has been one great tragedy in our immediate family, the death of our little daughter Ambika in 1968. Yet, in many ways, this haunting event has brought us closer together.

I have been fortunate in having caring brothers and sisters who have always believed in me and sustained me in good times and difficult days.

One is born to one's relatives, one chooses one's friends. Here again, fate has been kind. Over the years, many cherished and loyal companions have enlivened my life. Friendship, I believe, is a two-way path: you get as you give. I have tried to be as good to my friends as I would like them to be to me. With a few exceptions, I have been richly rewarded.

Looking back over sixty-six years, it seems as if I have been given a bountiful innings. Not everything, of course, has gone totally in the way I would have desired. But, then, I have genuinely looked at life as a matter of balance. Can anyone always have good times? Who wins every turn of the wheel of fortune? So much of what happens is beyond a man's making. So much is unexpected. The portion of our lives over which we have direct control is not as large as many think it is. I am not a fatalist. But I have seen too much to assume that everything which happens is entirely the result of one's personal actions. No man or woman is the sole arbiter of whatever befalls them.

This does not mean that we should abandon all to destiny. To my mind, being human implies a responsibility—an obligation to work at shaping our own fate. It has been said that God helps those who help themselves. I prefer the sentiment of the poet Iqbal, whose Urdu verses made a profound impression on me long ago:

> One must be so unselfish
> That when God writes your destiny
> He can be free to ask:
> What do you want?

In an individual's quests and aspirations values count. Throughout my own life, I have sought to act with a consistency reflecting the ideals to which my parents were so strongly committed. Their virtues were simple but clear: honesty, hard work, personal discipline, prudence and charity. These they did not proclaim and preach; they practised. Their example made an enduring impression on those around them. If I am able to communicate some of these values to my children and grandchildren, my life has been fulfilled and I will rest content.

For some years, I had been preparing for a kind of retirement at the age of sixty-five. And so, early in 1996, I handed over executive management of the Caparo Group to my sons. They have had long periods of preparation and it is for them to take our business into the future. For me, however, retirement does not mean inactivity. I look upon it more as a shift of interest—liberation to do the many things which active managerial duties did not allow.

One of these things which I had long promised myself was to participate more actively in public affairs. I have always believed that individuals owe something to the community and that, at some time in life, they should serve the common good. The question often is: how to do so? In my situation the decision was virtually made for me. Shortly after my retirement from active management I was appointed to the House of Lords. This has proven to be an engaging activity with many rewarding features.

Another commitment was to reflect on the unfolding of my own life—how a small boy from a rather remote part of a distant land eventually came to live in one of the great capitals of the world; how modest beginnings have evolved into considerable affluence; how the unknown son of a little-known family has been fortunate to meet and know some of the great and mighty men and women of our age. This book tells that story as I experienced it and tries to share the lessons I learned along the way.

Autobiographies are not usually written in a spirit of modesty. Few achievers, especially those whose accomplishments have been material, are given to humility. I am proud of what I have done in life. Yet, I also know that there are many areas in which I am a beginner—roads I am just exploring. Such new journeys do not start only from their commencement. That is why I am looking back as I look forward. In telling a story that I hope may prove instructive for others, I want to see what it has to teach me. This curiosity has overcome a long reluctance to record the events, motivations and reflections of a lifetime. But, then, this is also a fresh adventure . . .

SWRAJ PAUL

London
December 1997

1

Days of Childhood

India in 1931 was a land of brave men and courageous women. With few exceptions, they were prepared to sacrifice much in the hope of independence for their motherland. The measure of their heroism was that the prospect of freedom then looked so remote. The British were firmly in control of the country. Vast resources lay at their command. They were so confident of the future that a splendid new imperial capital had just been completed in New Delhi. Indian leaders could be imprisoned as and when it suited the convenience of the Raj. Even the most ardent supporters of a liberated India did not ever expect self-government within sixteen years. Yet, ordinary people were aroused by a spirit of nationalism which has rarely been seen in modern history. It was truly a moment of greatness.

It was into this world that I was born. The antecedents of the Paul family were in the present Indian state of Haryana, not too far from Delhi. They were simple people, farmers from the area around Hisar. The living was adequate. Several generations had settled there with little apparent interest in leaving their homestead. Even so, there must have been a spirit of enterprise or adventure in the time of my father's youth. Shortly before World War I, he and three of his brothers went to the city of Lahore to begin a business. Lahore, now in Pakistan, was then a large and prosperous city in the north of undivided India, about 200 miles away from their village.

In Lahore, they learned some of the rudiments of commerce. Coming from an agricultural background, this was a major break with tradition. Few individuals then did anything other than what their forebears had always done. After a while, in 1910, my father, Payare Lal, moved from Lahore to Jalandhar in Punjab. It was there that he began his own family and started a small manufacturing business. My mother, Mongwati, who was also from Haryana, was soon raising the older of the seven children she was to bear. Soon, my other uncles also moved to Jalandhar. They eventually lived in the same neighbourhood and engaged in identical businesses. It was quite a sight to see four siblings carrying on similar activities on virtually the same street without any rivalry or ill feeling, although they were in direct competition with each other.

In those days, around the 1920s, Jalandhar was a small town with a population of around fifty thousand. Although great national events were stirring and these inevitably affected the citizenry of Punjab, our life was normally quiet and conventional. My father was a producer of agricultural implements and sheet metal wares such as buckets, tubs and a variety of household items. The family lived and worked in one house—the living quarters were on the first floor, the factory and the office were on the ground floor, and a small steel-rolling mill was in the backyard. I really grew up above the shop!

At the time of my birth, in 1931, all of India was in ferment, aroused by Mahatma Gandhi's civil disobedience campaigns. These had created a great deal of excitement. The Salt March, the Mahatma's arrest and other happenings gave vigour to the Freedom Movement. A widely used slogan was 'We Want Swraj'. The literal meaning of swraj is, of course, freedom. To Indians of my age it had a much more symbolic resonance, combining the yearning for liberation with Gandhian virtues and an evocation of the spirit of India's past. My elder sister takes credit for naming me, but it was then almost natural that deeply nationalistic parents would want to give their sixth child the name Swraj.

I believe that an individual's emotional structure is largely lodged in his roots. The insecurities which often trouble men and women in later life reflect the atmosphere and relationships of their early youth. This may now be pop psychology, but it is also common sense. I was particularly fortunate to grow up in a close and caring family. My father was very proud of his expanding business. He was also very proud of his expanding family. We lived in the glow of that affection, a feeling made complete by the love of a gentle mother. Early childhood was happy and serene.

My father was not formally educated, but he was a wise man. He had a very clear sense of the values by which he lived and which he wanted his family to accept. Four of these became part of our daily routine—discipline, frugality, charity and unity. Reflecting on those days, I now realize that my father wanted his values to be part of our everyday habits and he arranged things in this way. There was little, if any, sermonizing and preachment. His truths had to be lived.

Father was a strong believer in discipline and work as a builder of discipline. Although he had deep affection for his children, he also made sure that each of us did some work. This was often some manual work so that our vanity would not be excessive and we would appreciate the dignity of any kind of labour. My elder brother Jit and I were assigned to sweep the office and the factory each day. We also did our daily household shopping, purchasing food and vegetables at the local bazaar. Waste and luxury were sinful to my father. He never denied us any necessities or basics, but like many good men in those days, he believed that frugality was a fundamental virtue and extravagance was ungodly. So, as children, we were only given two sets of clothes each—one to wear while the other was being washed.

Perhaps all this was excessive. We could have afforded a few more luxuries and comforts. Now we live in another age and our standards have changed.

The modern consumer world has infected us with the idea of instant gratification. In my own way, I, too, have probably been indulgent by my father's criteria. I still abhor needless extravagance, particularly of the ostentatious type, but I am probably more tolerant of the comforts of life than my father was. And, yet, as I look at the society we have built here, and are building in India, I feel that perhaps my father was right. The debilitating impact of unaffordable luxury has sapped many of the strengths we need to survive. The heedless way in which debt is accumulated to finance non-productive purchases is dangerous. Even more frightening is the long-term effect on our environment. There may come a day when my father's ethic of frugality will become mandatory for the survival of our planet.

Charity was very much a part of my father's culture. He strongly believed that any money which had been saved should be spent for the benefit of those in need. In front of our house, just outside the entrance, he erected a small stall. There was always something for anyone who passed by, often some grain or roasted peas. Many who could not afford to buy these requisites took them away from our stall. There was no accounting made, no reciprocity required and no obligation incurred. This notion of sharing some of the surplus has remained in our family to this day.

The entire family sat together for meals. It was my mother's special pleasure to serve us breakfast, lunch and dinner. She cherished these gatherings. It was an unwritten rule that everyone had to be present—a tradition which we continued long after her death.

The only exception was when we were at school and when my brother Jit, who began work in the business in 1939, had to be away. In fact, to say that any one of us began work is almost inaccurate. From childhood, we were associated with the business in some way or the other. They may have been minor duties, but we were all very much part of the enterprise and we took it seriously. As a young schoolboy I was drafted as an occasional typist and clerical assistant!

The first real shock in this peaceful existence came with my mother's death in childbirth. It was 1938 and I was barely seven years old. This terrible blow came without any warning. I still recall how we children were quickly removed to my uncle's house nearby in order not to expose us to most of the funeral ceremonies. I was too young to understand the meaning of it all, but I knew that something fatal had happened to my mother; something, I now know, easily preventable with contemporary medicine.

This was my first confrontation with the harshness of death. My mother was in her late thirties and was ever-present in my early childhood. Memories of her simple affection still linger. Once, when asked why she wore no jewellery, her reply said it all: 'My sons are my jewels.' The suddenness of her passing left us all with a feeling of abandonment. Since then, as many near and dear to me have departed, I have tried to understand this most fateful of human experiences. Many religions and philosophies offer explanations and consolations and often they help those who believe in them. Yet, to me, the randomness of death, especially when it touches those whose lives have not fully unfolded, defies comprehension. Its finality, its irrevocability, is so complete in a world where there is often a second chance. Perhaps one day we will be able to know more about the nature of death. Now, unsatisfactory as it is, we have just to accept it as everyone's destiny, beyond anyone's control. As my generation ages, these questions come closer and the answers are as distant as ever.

With my mother's death, the bond with my father seemed to increase. He had always been very fond of me; now we spent many more hours together. I shared his bedroom at night and, apart from school time, I was always with him. My elder sister, Prakash, looked after us and I became very attached to her. I was still a small boy when she married in 1941 and was so distraught at her leaving us that my father sent me to live with her for a little while in her new home.

In 1942, an event occurred which had a signal impact on me. It also tells much about those times. The eldest among my brothers is Bhaiji (Stya, pronounced Satya), who is twelve years my senior. He was, and is, a person of unusual courage. Afflicted with polio in infancy, he had to walk with crutches until surgically treated almost three decades later. Bhaiji's bravery was an inspiration. When in school, he even joined the hockey team. Despite his disability, he was the goalie and played with credit. In his teens and early twenties, Bhaiji was active in the Freedom Movement and participated in anti-colonial protests and demonstrations.

One day, our family was sitting around in the house when several policemen in plain clothes arrived and asked Bhaiji to come with them for a discussion. Hours passed and he did not return. My father organized a search. We were terrified, fearing the worst. Only on the following day did it become known that Bhaiji had been arrested under arbitrary laws called the Defence of India Rules. My father then went to see the Deputy Commissioner of Jalandhar, a British official in charge of the town. He was told that Bhaiji would be released if he could prevail upon his son to express regret and apologize for joining the Freedom Movement. My father refused. He would rather see his son in prison than make him compromise. Above all, he knew that whatever plea was made, Bhaiji himself would not yield.

In those days, men and women would suffer any hardship rather than dishonour their country. Families supported them and encouraged nationalist defiance. Individuals and groups forgot their differences and joined together. Against such determination, the British could do little. I often wonder what has happened to those qualities of unity and patriotism. Why has India lost them? Is it something which comes only once in the history of a nation and is then buried forever? Surely, a people capable of such extraordinary effort to gain freedom can harness this collective energy and sublime spirit to the task of nation-building. I fear that without a revival of such cooperation and dedication, India may not be able to make it. Policy, however enlightened, cannot substitute for this kind of commitment.

By the early 1940s, World War II had come to India. War, as wars often are, was good for business.

My father began manufacturing an expanded range of items. To make these products, which included milk cans and nuts and bolts, he had to construct a new factory. Jit, who was now fully engaged in our operations, was frequently in Calcutta dealing with the authorities, as steel had been brought under government control. After the war, he was to make Calcutta his home and still resides there. Profits were good and, in 1943, the family decided to buy a car. Until then, we children either walked or rode bicycles, while the elders used a horse-drawn buggy. Since even a ride in the buggy was a special event for the children, a car was an undreamed of wonder.

There were no car sales in Jalandhar. My father went to Lahore and purchased a second-hand Hudson for what seemed to be a huge amount of Rs. 3,000. At present rates of exchange, this is only about £60 or $100.* In those days, it was worth about thirty times more! Anyway, when my father returned in his car, we were one of only a handful of automobile owners in our town. It was a cause for much celebration for the whole family and a matter of pride for us all. The ownership of a vehicle in a small town then bestowed a kind of prestige which few enjoyed. Even my father, usually so austere in his ways, shared in the pleasure which his car brought.

Soon after this joyous event, tragedy struck. My uncle, Khemchand, died of heart failure. My father was especially close to this brother and the shock was

*Here and elsewhere, the amount conversions are based on exchange rates prevailing in 1996 when the bulk of this book was written.

unbearable. He rushed to Khemchand's house and broke down. Embracing the body, my father moaned in despair: 'You go, Khemchand, I'll bring you your meals.' None of us quite realized what this symbolized in his mind, but it was evident thereafter that he had lost any desire to live. He fell ill and, although he recovered, his last words to Khemchand seemed to haunt him. Often my father would say, almost as if speaking to himself, that he had not fulfilled this promise to his brother. There was no consolation for his grief.

About three months after the funeral of Khemchand, my father and I were alone together on our veranda. Jit was out of town. My sisters were in the kitchen. Suddenly, my father fell off the couch on which he was sitting. I raised the alarm and everyone gathered round. It was too late. He had died instantly. We never quite understood how intense our father's sorrow had been. Together with his sense of unfulfilled obligation, it had destroyed him. Such is the power of the human mind. He was only fifty-five.

The year was 1944. I was thirteen years old, but childhood had ended.

2

Early Youth

From childhood through adolescence to adulthood is a difficult passage for anyone. Innocence is eroded by awareness and then by knowledge. The protected fairyland in which most parents keep their children becomes exposed for what it is. In India then, and to some extent even now, the mores of society and parental love combined to insulate young people from the truths of life for as long as possible. Whether this sheltering, undertaken with the best of motives, is ultimately of any value is a subject of much debate. The artificial postponement of reality does perhaps make an eventual denouement shocking. On the other hand, I believe that the benefits of parental love at an early age overcome most of the drawbacks. It provides the reassurance essential for a growing child, especially in a harsh and confused contemporary world. Having known only a part of this caring, I can testify to how traumatic its absence can be.

To me, the decade after 1944 was agonizing. It began when I was thirteen, still somewhat immature for my age. We continued to live in what Indians call the joint family system, but the death of my parents created a terrible void. My brothers, Bhaiji and Jit, both several years older than me, did everything to ease this sorrow. They were the best of surrogate parents, providing the emotional and material security so necessary for a young boy. At the same time, their stewardship of the family enterprises was proving increasingly successful.

Jit, particularly, was beginning to show the financial genius which has since made him one of India's outstanding businessmen.

Bhaiji, who later in life devoted much of his energy to developing quality education in India, was particularly concerned about my schooling. I attended a primary institution within walking distance of our home and, as the years went by, my academic record was quite good. When I matriculated from this school in 1945, Bhaiji insisted that I enrol at Foreman Christian College in Lahore. He felt that this would provide me with better instruction than that which was available locally. It would give me insight into a wider world and offer opportunities not possible in Jalandhar.

In those days, Bhaiji's approach was unusually far-sighted. Families engaged in commerce usually gave their children a basic education and brought them into business as soon as possible. Experience was regarded as much more valid than learning in this kind of career. The pursuit of a university degree was uncommon and would have given considerable amusement to the commercial classes of that time. How things have changed—and I am certain for the better. In an age when business is so international, there are few alternatives to the perspectives that universities engender. However, I have also seen too many whiz-kids, fresh with MBA and other degrees, make elementary mistakes which ruin their employers.

While the training which higher education provides is invaluable, education must be a supplement, not a substitute, for common sense. Experience is itself a rare form of knowledge which academia alone cannot provide. The problems of experience are of another nature: the older we get, the greater our tendency to convert experience into irrelevant nostalgia. What we need from experience is less reminiscence and more service to the community!

I attended Foreman Christian College for two years. I had never been away from home before, and yearned to go back. But, somehow, I managed to reconcile to circumstances. Regular trips to Jalandhar on Sundays or visits by the family relieved a little of the homesickness. What helped a lot was the kindness of our American principal and his wife. Dr and Mrs Rice were Christian missionaries who were committed educators. They became fond of me and were a source of great inspiration. Mrs Rice was the sister of the President of Massachusetts Institute of Technology in Boston. This was, and is, one of America's finest centres of advanced scientific and engineering studies.

Mrs Rice urged me to go abroad and join MIT. Under her guidance I began to explore the possibilities of admission.

Yet, this was an unlikely prospect. My brothers and I were anxious that I pursue engineering because this knowledge would be useful for our business.

They knew that technology was changing and if our enterprises were to progress they needed more scientific input. But the cost of studying abroad was prohibitive, so it was always assumed I would enter an Indian institution. America was so distant that it was almost a mirage.

Suddenly, everything was shaken by the terrible events which descended on India. In 1947, the British withdrew and their subcontinental empire was partitioned. Lahore would now belong to Pakistan. Overnight, I became a foreigner in another country as the old Punjab, in which Lahore and Jalandhar were subsumed, was split between India and Pakistan. Murderous riots exploded and continued uncontrolled on both sides of the new border. Assaults on Hindus were taking place all around me in Lahore. In great panic, I was able to clamber aboard a train to make the hundred-mile journey back to Jalandhar. It was the last train to get through unscathed. After this, Hindus seeking to escape by rail were dragged from their coaches and massacred. I had been extraordinarily lucky.

This was a moment of madness and the divided Punjab was at the heart of it. Hindu refugees streamed into the Indian Punjab from across the Pakistan frontier. Huge camps were organized to accommodate them in miserable conditions. They brought tragic tales of deprivation, killings, loss of families and properties. Feelings were so inflamed that retaliatory anti-Muslim outrages erupted.

Being close to the border, Jalandhar was badly affected. There was little anyone could do. Several of our Muslim friends were butchered—murders that defy description. To go to their aid was instant death; to stand helpless was a horrible admission of powerlessness and inadequacy. I was sixteen and my world was in flames.

The scars of those harrowing experiences have remained with a whole generation of Indians and, I suppose, Pakistanis. An emotional wall, its foundations laid in blood, separates peoples who lived together in relative calm for centuries. Who can say whether the partition of British India was a mistake? Nonetheless, it created two antagonistic states that spend vast amounts on weapons of war rather than using this money for development. Must everyone with memories of 1947 die before a sensible accommodation between India and Pakistan can be reached? It will be worse if these nightmares have become an inheritance implanted in the national consciousness of both countries. For those of us who knew undivided India, where anyone could easily travel from Khyber to Dacca and from Kashmir to Kanyakumari (then Cape Comorin), this is a consummate tragedy. It seems that what politics and diplomacy have separated cannot be repaired by the same means. Do we have to wait for generals or saints to solve these problems? Since neither is likely to succeed, are we condemned to unending hostility?

The terrors which I witnessed often come back to me. Nobody had anticipated these outbursts. They happened overnight. How quickly the sickness spreads when evil is unleashed! I saw normally sensible and kindly people turn into monsters who relished destruction and mutilated their victims. Is the skin of civilization so thin that men can so quickly become savages? To anyone alive in India in 1947, Bosnia and Rwanda and similar situations are no surprise. To me, a more disturbing question arises: Are we always to go on like this?

Turbulence in Punjab continued through 1947. The refugees, their miseries and their reactions had a bitter impact. Confusion and disorder prevailed. Schools were closed for almost a year and students were asked to undertake social work in the camps. We worked twenty hours a day and more. It was a melancholy yet strangely uplifting task. The sights were tormenting but it was gratifying to know that our labours made a difference to the lives of desolate people. It is here that I first began to appreciate the value of community service, an ethic that has influenced my own life. And it was here that I first saw Jawaharlal Nehru and was witness to his greatness. At the onset of turmoil the recently appointed Prime Minister toured the troubled areas. Everywhere he went, Nehru appealed for calm and peace. It was an appeal couched in unusual language. He demanded that the violence stop. He forcefully admonished the people, scolding them for what they had done.

I felt the ambivalence of the mass response. They

loved Nehru, but they did not like his message. There was a reaction of both affection and anger in the camps. After all, he was calling for restraint when revenge was the foremost emotion. Nehru himself showed no regard for the erosion of his popularity. He refused to pander. It was in the character of this man to do what he thought was correct for his country. His first instinct was that of the statesman; politics was secondary. This is why the youth of my era so admired Jawaharlal and why other leaders seem so small compared with him. Watching the Prime Minister, I could not have imagined that fate would bring me in close contact with his family many years later.

Things finally quietened with the assassination of Mahatma Gandhi in January 1948. His death was a soul-searing shock. Gandhi had been such an influence that most of us thought of him as a permanent presence. The way in which he was killed caused a wave of shame. Here was Bapu, the father and conscience of independence, slaughtered in public. How sad it is that it took the horror of this act to bring an end to the collective killings. What Gandhi had struggled, often unsuccessfully, to do in life was accomplished by his death. Men of peace frequently meet bloody ends: this is one of the less dignifying truths of history. There is a corollary that is equally disturbing for South Asia. Why is an area which is the home of profound messages of peace so infused with violence? Why have so many of the region's leaders met death by assassination? Unless there is much more introspection, these awful spasms will eventually destroy the spiritual ethos of the subcontinent.

There was now no question of returning to Lahore. When education resumed in Jalandhar, I attended Doaba College and graduated in 1949 with honours in mathematics, physics and chemistry. There was exciting news from MIT. I was accepted for admission in the autumn of 1949. At first, I was reluctant to tell my brothers. I thought they would be discouraging. It would cost too much to go to America and study there. The financial burdens would be too heavy and the separation too far and too long. Nobody in our family had travelled out of the country. But, to my surprise, Bhaiji and Jit were delighted. They urged, indeed insisted, that I proceed to the United States for higher studies.

Another adventure began. I had not journeyed further than Lahore in my life, and the rush and strangeness of it all was intimidating. I went to Delhi to get my visa and in late summer boarded the Jalandhar–Bombay train. My departure was a big occasion for our family and friends. About three hundred of them assembled at the railway station to say goodbye. It was as if a major celebrity was leaving town rather than a nervous teenager! Amidst tears and cheers, I departed. Never have I received such a send-off!

From Bombay, I flew to London where my brothers had business connections. In five days, I had quite an experience. Checking into the Great Eastern Hotel, I sought to explore this unknown world. Gradually, I realized that British men and women who lived in their homeland were remarkably different from those who ruled the Empire. These were ordinary, unaffected and helpful people. They had none of the airs and imperious manners of their kith and kin in India. The colonial Englishman acquired a style that was supposed to indicate his superiority over the natives. It may have impressed a few; it offended many. Perhaps the most lasting aspect of this artificial performance, with all its petty social rituals, was on the practitioners themselves. Back home in Britain, after years of colonial service, they found themselves singularly out of place and unable to adjust to the civilities of normal existence.

I visited two of our commercial contacts. Mr Stephen Kay of Stewarts & Lloyds sent me to see their factory in Glasgow. What I really saw was only rain and my recollections of that city are very watery ones. In order to inspire my academic efforts, Mr Ricketts, a family friend, told me of some financial strains which my family were undergoing. I was unaware of the particular situation that he discussed. He, too, was unaware that it had been concealed from me. Apparently the manager of our Bombay office had gambled heavily and indebted the company in order to pay his personal losses. Bhaiji and Jit paid these obligations in full, but this had put our business in a perilous condition. They had not disclosed anything, fearing that it would deter me from going abroad.

Overwhelmed with distress and thoughts of home, I informed Jit that I was returning at once. Using the balance of my ticket, I took the first available flight to Bombay. All I wanted to do was to help my family and cease to be a financial burden on them. Jit came to meet me at the airport. After listening to my outpourings for about an hour, he calmly said that I was booked on the next plane out to Boston. There was no argument possible and so I was back on my way to America. In retrospect, I will always be grateful to Jit for his good-humoured but implacable insistence. The MIT experience proved to be one of the turning points in my life.

The following four years, until 1953, were spent at MIT. Initially, I was unhappy in these alien surroundings. I lived in the university dormitory and kept much to myself. Asians were little known in Boston in those days. At MIT there were only seven others from India. Whenever we travelled around America and said we were Indians, the inevitable question was: 'To which tribe do you belong?' One of the by-products of my isolation was immersion in study. As a result, my grades were excellent. Slowly, the ice began to break. In large part, this was due to a generous and supportive faculty who extended themselves to welcome foreign students.

This made it much easier to fit in. I began participating in a variety of campus activities and adapted well to my new environment.

Around those years, American universities had a huge and exceptional intake of older students. This was the consequence of the GI Education Program, a government-funded scheme to reward soldiers and other veterans of World War II. They were very serious students, many were married, and much more mature than the average undergraduate. Their presence and their unabashed informality had a positive influence on all of us. In contrast to what I had expected, these military men were exceptionally compassionate towards their younger colleagues. Wars are supposed to harden and brutalize those who participate in them, but here was proof that they could also humanize.

University life in those days was very different from what it is now. There was much less focus on wider concerns and radical causes. Interest in outside affairs centred on issues such as anti-colonialism and the start of the civil rights movement. Gender, environment, multiculturalism and ethnicity, human and gay rights were nowhere on the agenda. By today's standards this was a very limited docket. The central purpose of student life was to learn, to graduate and to become gainfully employed quickly thereafter. Yet, towards the end of my stay, harsher rumblings heralded the coming storms. The overtones of McCarthyism reached Boston, and Harvard was especially scourged by it. Ill winds were blowing, but my years were calm and untroubled.

MIT helped to develop my personality. The constant interaction with people from other cultures was enormously broadening. The intellectual challenges were stimulating and provoked much discussion and debate. The sociability of American boys and girls was infectious. A sense of self-confidence began to grow. The university was famed for its rigorous standards and this generated a 'can do' attitude. Every challenge should be met, every problem could be solved, all doors would open to those who knocked hard enough. It was a demanding culture and its impact still lingers in me! Because I was anxious not to overload my family, I sought as many temporary jobs as I could find. At various times, I was a waiter, a research assistant and a college instructor. When I graduated, my savings were sufficient to buy a car which I took to India.

Today, large numbers of Indian students attend American universities. Most of them have superior academic records. It concerns me deeply that many of these young people are more fixated on style and taste than on having any work experience. Generous allowances from home enable the cultivation of a 'hip' or 'mod' lifestyle. It is an old-fashioned belief, but I strongly feel that every foreign undergraduate should engage in some full or part-time employment. There is no better way to understand another society than by working in it. Affluent parents unwittingly do a disservice to their offspring by providing too many comforts and insulating them from reality.

Children are sent for higher education abroad without giving much thought to character-building. And then, we are aghast when things go wrong.

In 1952, I was awarded both a bachelor's and master's degree by MIT. Within the next year, I completed the course requirements for a doctoral award. It was my intention to go to India, work for a while and come back for completion of my dissertation. Around that time, my brother Bhaiji came to Boston for medical attention. He was in hospital for close to six months. A series of protracted surgeries took place. One day, in an attempt to cheer him up, we drove to Concord Park nearby. Bhaiji was seated on a bench, and appeared deeply depressed. A stranger walked up and asked why he looked so miserable. Bhaiji explained that his leg was partially paralysed due to childhood polio and that the treatment was long and painful. To our amazement, the bypasser loosened his clothing and showed us that both his arms and both his legs were artificial. He told Bhaiji to be grateful that only one of his legs was afflicted!

This incident was a remarkable morale booster. It gave Bhaiji an enormous psychological lift. The treatment was also working well. Gradually, he was able to walk on two legs for the first time since infancy. It was thrilling to see him stand erect without assistance. We left for India in a joyful mood. I was looking forward to a short sojourn at home and then returning to finish my doctorate. But, once again, the unexpected intervened, and it was not to be.

3

Return to India

We arrived in India brimful of confidence in March 1953. The country was in a paradoxical condition. The afterglow of independence kindled widespread feelings of patriotism and commitment. Public life reflected the enthusiasm and principles of the struggle for liberty. There was a genuine willingness to accept short-term sacrifices in order to create a nation which would be strong, free and prominent in the world community. There was hardly any corruption and high expectations from the future. Yet, there was also a kind of continuing enslavement. We were politically self-governing but still monopolized by British rules, regulations, commercial standards and economic ties. The mentality of the bureaucracy, the holdover of the imperial Indian Civil Service, particularly reflected this duality: honest and honestly wanting to build a new India, yet unable to envision that anything not British could be first-rate.

I lived in India for the next thirteen years and saw much of this change. For me, personally, it was an exciting period. Apeejay, as the family business was called, expanded exponentially. From a moderate enterprise we grew into a network of companies with branches and facilities around the country. We entered several new fields and laid the foundations for what has since become one of the larger and most stable commercial groups in India.

Bhaiji, Jit and I were later joined by our youngest brother, Surrendra, an energetic and convivial personality who contributed so significantly to our activities until his tragic death—he was assassinated by Assamese rebels in 1990. The Paul brothers worked smoothly as a team, our complementary skills enabling the effective management of increasingly diverse operations.

During this decade or so, the national economic environment began to deteriorate. Much of the vigour and idealism of the immediate post-independence period gradually drained away. With the best of motives, a quasi-socialist framework was imposed on the economy. Planning became the watchword of policy and government-owned enterprises were expected to be engines of growth. Red tape breeds red tape and an encroaching Licence Raj with its permits, controls and allocated quotas began to steadily stifle economic dynamism. Administered by bureaucrats, many of whom sincerely thought that these were the answers to India's needs, this system strangled the entrepreneurial talents for which Indians are known worldwide. Confiscatory taxation led to a parallel economy and the black market rivalled the open market. Influence-peddling and corruption became endemic, and politicians and their intermediaries were quick to seize these opportunities. Worst of all, a culture of dependency was woven between the private sector and government.

A closed circle of political notables, senior public servants and state-supported tycoons brought untold and unfair benefits to all within its ambit. But the country was cheated. Only within the past five years has the failure of this behemoth compelled a reconsideration and provoked reforms. Slaying the dragon is currently proving more difficult than anyone could envisage.

This litany of woes is, of course, retrospective. It was not all that bad at the start. Back in Jalandhar, I was again working with the family. My first assignment was to join my brother-in-law Kalwant Rai on a construction project. One of the showpieces of independent India was to be a new capital for Punjab designed by French architect Le Corbusier. We had received a contract for the sanitation pipeline grid and Kalwant Rai supervised it. The elegant urban complex of Chandigarh was a vast site of rubble and holes in the ground when I first saw it. For an MIT graduate, a labour camp with distant outdoor toilets was quite a culture shock! It was my introduction to Indian business and it took a while to adapt. After two months, there was little more I could do, so, in late 1953, I went to join Jit in Calcutta. Here I was to remain for the rest of my life in India.

By this time, Jit had established a steel tubes import business. India was producing only limited amounts of steel and Jit purchased substantial amounts of foreign tubing which was then shipped to Calcutta. His service centre in the city warehoused these products and sold them for use in public works and industry. It was a tough and tedious activity—the profit margin was set by the government and everything was subject to its approval. The steel controller, an important bureaucrat, had to authorize each import licence and only British standard specifications were acceptable. If steel was not made according to these standards import permission was refused. There was no sense in this tyranny of specifications; it existed simply because it had always existed and the bureaucracy was just unwilling to alter it. Ironically, even Britain purchased steel with different specifications from continental Europe. Only India insisted that any imported steel, wherever it was made, had to conform to British standards. This rigid imposition of British criteria extracted a heavy cost. India was losing the economic benefits of buying equally good but cheaper steel made to equivalent specifications elsewhere in the world.

I saw this as absurdly outmoded and also as a potential opportunity. With Jit's support, and his wide access to officialdom, I set out to change things.

The resistance was unbelievable. Layer after layer of civil servants adamantly refused to consider any other standards, including those of continental Europe, as equal to British ones. Finally, I did change their minds, and it was my American education which helped. Not only was I able to present irrefutable technical evidence, but my MIT degree was apparently as convincing as my scientific data! The single specification rule was broken. Less costly steel was at last available to India. As for our own business, we were now free to import European tubing at much lower prices. It was my first success in the commercial world but it foreshadowed many future tangles with the bureaucracy.

Another interesting incident, which had an uplifting impact on our business, then occurred. In 1953, there was a global shortage of steel tubing and it was a struggle to obtain supplies. Jit had to travel back and forth searching for sources in Europe. While he was away, I was in charge of our operations. One morning, a casually dressed Eastern European gentleman walked into my office. In those days, a jacket and tie was like a calling card: it assured respectability in the business community! This informal individual announced himself as the Deputy Trade Representative of the Soviet Union in Calcutta. He asked if we wanted to buy steel tubes from Russia.

To the ears of anyone conversant with international trade this sounded like a joke—steel from Russia was laughable. Still, my visitor persisted. So I suggested a price of about 20 per cent below world rates and said we would buy two thousand tons if he could meet it. Thereupon, the visitor, Mr Vasiliev, went away and I gave the matter no more thought.

Five days later, Vasiliev showed up again bringing with him something like a purchase contract drafted on an ordinary sheet of paper. Partly unbelieving and partly amused, I signed the scruffy document and put my copy away. To my mind, this was all so obscure and ridiculous that I did not even mention it to my brother on his return. Suddenly, three months later, a cablegram arrived saying that 500 tons of steel tubing was ready for shipment from the Soviet Union and requesting that a letter of credit be obtained to guarantee payment. This was serious business.

Once again, we were captives of prejudice. Indian institutions did not then transact foreign exchange and our international banker was Lloyds Bank. Mr Tebbit, the General Manager, was shocked at my request for a credit of £30,000 for the Soviet Union. Steel from Russia did not seem credible. After referral to his head office, Tebbit said he could only allow £5,000 and that, too, as a special concession to a very good client! Nobody else would do any better.

I took the dilemma to Vasiliev, who said he would get back to me. Soon, he asked me to call at the Bank of China, which had a small branch in Calcutta, and meet a Mr Chi. That was the era of Sino-Soviet cordiality and Mr Chi, a former student at Harvard University who knew MIT well, was willing to undertake the transaction. And so, the initial shipment of Russian steel arrived in India.

In January 1954, I was the first Indian business visitor to the Soviet Union. For four weeks, I travelled through the country and enjoyed exceptional hospitality. We concluded a purchase agreement at prices much under the world market. Apeejay, which had bought only steel tubing prior to this, now began to import all types of steel. Through these Soviet contacts, supplies from Eastern Europe were available to us and we were given an exclusive arrangement with them. Another extended battle with the steel control authorities ensued, their technical departments even suggesting that Russian steel billets would crack when processed in India. Thanks to Jit's way with people, and my technical knowledge, this dispute ended happily. Apeejay was now a major factor in Indian steel and our profits reflected this progress. What is more, India was able to obtain many advantages because of competition among suppliers, something which did not exist before our East European ventures.

Another fortuitous happening led Apeejay into the shipping business. In 1959, on a flight from Delhi to Calcutta, I was seated beside Dr Nagendra Singh, then Director-General of Shipping in the Government of India. Dr Singh, who later became an eminent member of the International Court of Justice, told me that the government was anxious to develop a national cargo fleet. He said a lot of assistance was available. I did not initially pay much attention to our conversation. Shortly thereafter, I was in Germany to meet one of our steel suppliers. Willi Schleiker had a controversial background. He was a key Nazi steel executive during the war and was imprisoned by the Allies. Released to help in the economic rehabilitation of Germany, Schleiker soon rebuilt his own fortune. We usually met at his offices in Dusseldorf, but on this occasion he suggested I come to Hamburg where he had recently bought a shipyard. When I discussed

Indian shipping, Schleiker offered me a second-hand vessel whose owners could not pay their repair bill to him. I immediately cabled Dr Nagendra Singh. Promptly came a reply offering government support for the purchase. This was the origin of the Apeejay Shipping Line which is now a well-known freight carrier. In 1960 I was proud to see the Apeejay flag amast the first Indian ship to sail through the St Lawrence Seaway into the Great Lakes of North America.

I was enjoying the excitement and challenges of the business world. I had taken over management of the international part of our steel operations, while Jit handled the domestic side. We interacted exceptionally well and his rare acumen was an enormous asset. For more than a decade, I travelled abroad for several months each year negotiating steel purchases. I came to know most foreign producers and was familiar with the topography of numerous mills, especially in Europe. The steel industry there has consolidated and most of these facilities have closed. However, in the post-war years they were the backbone of Europe's economy. My trips created other opportunities for expansion, some fruitful and some less so. Apeejay was not only importing steel, we were now manufacturing it. Real estate, hotels, pharmaceuticals and confectionary were among our other interests. The little cottage industry of Payare Lal from Jalandhar had come a long way!

In these years, the contours of modern industry were emerging. They eventually evolved into the structure which largely defines the Indian industrial economy today. One category of enterprise—state-owned corporations—was created with the objective of bringing the spirit of nationalism to the larger tasks of economic development. These corporations were given virtual monopolies in their areas of business because it was expected that they would operate in the public interest.

In the 1950s they performed exceptionally well. There were two reasons for this: political interference was minimal, and management was in the hands of men of outstanding integrity and vision who were committed to industrial modernization.

As time went by, several changes undermined and distorted the original mission. The 1960s were a turning point: many outstanding managers departed because they would not tolerate interference. The meddling of politicians began to increase; any significant decision, and many insignificant ones, now became subject to ministerial orders. Supine administrators were installed to carry them out. Corruption began to be noticeable, although not so endemic as in the 1970s and after. Subservience, not competence, became the preferred criteria for management, and any concept of public accountability virtually disappeared. Monopoly became a smokescreen to cover up inefficiency. Consequently, despite protected markets, the results of these enterprises steadily declined to their present pathetic showing. Extension of the state sector in the 1960s—the nationalization of insurance and banks, the creation of more state financial institutions—was also initiated with laudable motives. The intent was to make their capital resources and services available to many more than the favoured few who had hitherto enjoyed them. Here, too, political control and intrusion extracted a heavy toll and this expansion has ultimately proven self-defeating.

There is nothing inherently wrong with the notion of state-owned industries if they can be free of political tinkering and managed by able executives who are guided by results, individuals who are dedicated, incorruptible and not subservient. Unfortunately, such persons are rare to find and not welcome to public service in India and many other developing countries. State-owned enterprises fail for the same reasons that communism and Gandhian approaches have failed. At both leadership and citizen levels, it has been impossible to transform human nature so as to produce the selfless new socialist man of Marx, or the self-denying Gandhian of pre-independence India. Such noble attributes of character do arise under special circumstances, revolutionary pressures or freedom struggles. In more normal situations, however, this ethic of altruism does not seem to prevail on a large scale. Indian governments sought to compensate, to make sure that the national interest was foremost and that abuses would not happen, by wrapping the whole system in an enormous thicket of rules and regulations. This morass of ordinances, licences and permits only spawned a controlled economy tangled in red tape and a breed of fixers who manipulated the web for their benefit.

Currently, there is much talk of privatizing state-owned operations and government monopolies. Two fresh dangers loom. First, valuable public properties can be sold at bargain prices to friendly buyers. Second, the sale of public monopolies to private investors may result in even more oppressive private monopolies. The best way in which to serve the civic good is to allow competition to break or erode all monopolies and to broadbase divested ownership. Then, alert shareholders will demand accountability from managements and scrutinize operations for any irregularities. In modern society, where idealism alone appears insufficient incentive for lawful corporate behaviour, there is no substitute for this kind of transparency.

In the environment brought about by controls and regulations, a second kind of enterprise began to flourish. These were larger companies in the private sector who now found it easy to make profits by pleasing the regulators—the bureaucracy—and greasing their pathway. Competitive skills and efficiencies became unnecessary or secondary in allocated and protected markets. In addition, the expansion of public financial institutions, their virtual monopoly of large-scale investment capitals, their increasing investments in these companies, and the conversion of their loans into equity made them dominant shareholders. Favoured managements could keep their positions and their perquisites with little personal financial interest, as long as they had the blessings of the institutional shareholders.

As long as the institutions were happy, performance did not matter very much. And if managements were criticized by these institutions, which they rarely were, there was always recourse to political influence—the ministries bossed the institutions and the politicos bossed the ministries!

An example of this was exposed in 1983, when I challenged the managements of two of the biggest industrial houses in India. At that time, the Shri Ram family owned only 10 per cent of DCM's 8,025,272 equity shares of Rs. 25 each. Government insurance companies, development banks and unit trusts held 42.5 per cent of equity shares. Similarly, the Nanda family owned less than 5 per cent of Escorts' 13,377,208 equity shares of Rs. 10 each. Public institutions owned 54.9 per cent of these equity shares. The Shri Rams and the Nandas had managed these businesses for decades with very poor results but with plenty of perks and few questions asked. Invariably, the institutions and their board nominees sided with these politically influential family managements. Smaller shareholders had no say. And things just continued as they were until my intervention. But more of that later.

This pampered coterie of favoured industrialists were given highly preferential access to government handouts. Their companies became a kind of extension of the state but without even the limited scrutiny that government corporations are occasionally subject to. Their talents were not managerial or creative but well honed in the arts of cultivating and persuading officials and power-holders. In a truly dynamic business context they would have been pygmies; in a protected economy they were giants! Worst of all, by their stranglehold on sources of credit and on the licence system, they inhibited the advancement of small and medium-sized Indian businesses, enterprises which are quite effectively operated because the owners utilize their own capital, and you do not steal from yourself! What chance have most of these smaller entrepreneurs against an establishment which can, almost at will, make and break deals, sabotage competition and tilt the playing field to suit its convenience?

I first bumped into this establishment in my Calcutta days. In the early 1960s, I negotiated a collaboration agreement with the famed global cosmetics corporation Revlon. We had to secure permission from the Government of India for this project. Things were moving well and there were a few adjustments which the authorities requested. Suddenly, at the behest of a leading local cosmetics manufacturer, every possible obstacle was placed in the way of our proposal.

Despite my strenuous submissions, we were finally told that clearance would be granted on only one condition—that we did not use the Revlon name, logo or trademark! In the meanwhile, my antagonists approached Revlon with offers just the opposite of mine. They provided assurances of government approval for all the things they had objected to when I made them, and even threw in a one-half share of equity at no cost to Revlon! Somehow, the firebrand socialist leader Krishna Menon, then an important member of the Cabinet, heard about this and ended everything! Another joint venture which I sponsored, between Sheraton Inns and Apeejay, for a modern hotel in Calcutta, was also undermined, this time by the biggest Indian hoteliers. It was a one-sided game loaded against those who dared to impinge on the reservations of the establishment, shelters well guarded for them by the bureaucracy!

While all these happenings were going on, my personal happiness was complete. In 1956, I married Aruna Vij, a charming lady from Calcutta. We met by chance at a social occasion and were so drawn to each other that we married in a week. Our home was blessed with twin boys, Ambar and Akash, in December 1957. By Aruna's choice, the names of all our five children begin with the letter A, why I have still not found out! A daughter, Anjli, was born in 1959. With a growing family and vigorous business, there was much to be thankful for.

4

Ambika

The story of Ambika is an inexplicable tragedy. It unfolded over five years but its memory remains undiminished. For three decades I have tried to search for some meaning to these events. I am still searching. Perhaps, there are certain experiences in life whose inner truths will always be veiled— occurrences whose sensibility cannot be penetrated by logic and rational inquiry. All I can say is that this sequence of happenings indelibly affected my being. That it did, I know. How it did so is difficult to explain. When sorrow is so personal an emotion, how can the core of each individual's anguish be fully shared? Nonetheless, because of its conditioning impact on my life and career, I will recount the general features of this episode.

Our fourth child was born on 12 November 1963,

the same day as our older daughter. Ambika was an enchanting child, lively and intelligent beyond her years. She captivated everyone with whom she came into contact. Now, it seems as if she had an angelic personality—almost too ethereal to be of this world. Then, she was an especially engaging little girl whose life proceeded rather conventionally until she was two years of age. About that time, she began having occasional spells of fever and listlessness. The doctors in Calcutta did not consider this very serious, putting her problems down to the usual ailments of small children.

Because these spells were disturbingly frequent, I wrote to a medical friend in New York describing the symptoms. Dr Clarence Cohen replied suggesting a variety of tests, particularly to eliminate any possibility of leukaemia. The tests were completed and the doctors in Calcutta again advised that there was nothing dangerous. In contrast, Dr Cohen, who had seen the results, told me that his diagnosis confirmed leukaemia and suggested treatment abroad. We decided to go immediately.

In 1966, there were highly restrictive controls on foreign travel out of India. Only one family member could accompany a patient. But Ambika's condition required that both Aruna and I go with her. We faced a frightening series of regulatory obstacles. After much effort, securing a series of documents and establishing precedents, I was able to make a case for both parents to travel. A strike by the Reserve Bank of India staff threatened to delay our departure, but an understanding Deputy Controller of Foreign Exchange in Calcutta wrote out the special permit in his own hand. We left the same day.

We arrived in London in September 1966. Ambika was treated at the Middlesex Hospital. We were told that her illness was fatal. There was no cure. But we kept praying for a miracle to happen. We lived on hope and it was this faith which enabled me to function with a semblance of normality. Each new medication induced a remission which would last for a while.

Our spirits would rise. Then would come the bad news of another relapse.

These devastating blows were made all the more poignant by Ambika's behaviour. She was cheerful and positive, quite unable to understand her terrible medical state. I had rented a flat close to the hospital, the same premises in which we still live, and Aruna and I took turns at her bedside. Aruna spent the day there, while I sat by my daughter each night. The course of leukaemia weakens its victim as it progresses, but these downslides are interspersed with temporary improvements. The invalid then appears to recover fully and can carry on a regular existence.

So, poor Ambika was periodically in hospital but out and about at other times. She was able to go to school occasionally. We tried to lighten her days by taking her to the London Zoo nearby. This was a source of special pleasure for her—the animals and birds gave her a thrill. It was heart-warming to watch how spiritedly she played at the zoo, how great was her enjoyment in these pleasant natural surroundings. In the early 1990s I was able to assist this zoo to recover from financial setbacks that threatened closure, and to help rebuild it. Today, a statue of Ambika, set in the midst of a pool and water fountain, graces its central patio—a most appropriate memorial that was dedicated on her birthday in 1994.

A few months into our stay in London, a twist of fate brought about my first direct contact with Prime Minister Indira Gandhi. Our other three children had been left behind in Calcutta. Their Christmas holidays were coming and they were anxious to be with Aruna and me. We, too, missed them very much. According to government rules they could not come over—such were the restrictions of that time. We were desolate. As a last recourse, I wrote a long and personal letter to the Prime Minister explaining the difficulties of our situation. Soon, the wheels of officialdom began turning. Arrangements were made to satisfy the legal requirements and our family was united again. This was one of those frequent acts of kindness which Mrs Gandhi undertook, unknown to the public and in conflict with her stern image. Behind the iron carapace was a very human woman who did not often allow that side of her nature to be visible. For reasons best known to herself, Indira Gandhi rather feared that disclosure of her humanity would be mistaken for weakness or exploited as a vulnerability by her opponents.

The year 1967 was a tortuous one lightened by fragments of happiness. Ambika was often in hospital. Each occasion when she emerged brought us some hope. She was quite serene. We prayed together for her improvement. In her childlike handwriting she drafted small letters to God asking for blessings. We took her to the holy shrine at Lourdes. For a while she was remarkably vigorous, but then relapsed again. Lourdes became associated with wellness in her mind. As she entered hospital for the last time, she asked to be taken there again.

We had become so close that I could almost feel her moods, her pains and her joys. This was not so much a physical reaction as it was emotional and psychic empathy. Slowly, Ambika drifted into a worsening condition. The helplessness of it all was unbearable. What can torment a father more than watching life ebb from a little daughter whom he has brought into the world? No child should ever predecease a parent. This is only wishfulness. It is, unfortunately, not the way of things.

Until the final moments, we sustained hope. Just before the end the doctors administered an experimental drug which had promise of prolonging life. Once again, we held our breaths and prayed. It was to no avail. Ambika's passing in 1968 left me shattered. What was the use of intelligence, money, position and all the assets which the world values when nothing could save a loved one? I lost all interest in work and even in daily life. Despair has a numbing effect. *Sanyas*—withdrawal into a period of spiritual reflection and contemplation—was all I could do. My brothers and our whole family tried hard to console me. Without this support, I would not have survived or been able to confront the questions which haunted me.

A period of introspection followed. I began to

wonder about the direction of life. Aruna and I thought we should stay in London for a while. After all, it was where Ambika had died. Our other children were enrolled in school here and doing well. After about eighteen months, a sense of reconciliation began to grow. Over and over again, a thought recurred: 'Swraj, you were not meant to do nothing.' I had a choice: go back to India where our family business was flourishing or to start afresh. Aruna and I decided to make a new beginning and a new home in England. We had too many recent remembrances to leave and there were distracting opportunities and challenges. We refused to be defeated.

Gradually, from this tragedy, another life dawned. Tentatively, with many hesitations and misgivings, I returned to work. In small steps and incremental advances, Caparo came into being. Through all this, Ambika remains a continuing memory—a being that was never fulfilled, a love that was cruelly cut down, an angel who changed my life. I wish it were otherwise but maybe this was the course of destiny. Perhaps our way of perceiving death should not be so conclusive. The great Hindu sacred text, the Bhagavad Gita, puts it this way:

> If the slayer thinks he slays
> Or the slain thinks he is slain
> Both know not the truth of life
> Because neither he slays nor he is slain.

5

Building Caparo

Deep sorrow does not really leave anyone whom it has touched. However, different individuals react in different ways. To some, it is a paralysing agony which psychologically incapacitates and causes a withdrawal. This is what initially happened to me after Ambika's passing. Yet, after a while, I began to feel that profound sadness was not meant to dominate my emotions. It is too spiritually pretentious to suggest that there was divine guidance in my reactions. Yet, it now seems as if I was somehow inspired to find solace in work.

And so, I gradually began to occupy myself in business. It was a slow and uneven process but my interest revived and increased. The regular routine of the office, the involvement and the responsibilities were a deflection from the total absorption which sorrow imposes. Quite naturally, I looked to the steel industry. I did not have any capital but I was well acquainted with this business and knew many people in it. Buying and selling steel was logical. I did just that—purchasing steel in Europe, selling it in Britain; buying steel in the United States, selling it in Europe and wherever else I could. It was entirely a one-man operation conducted from a room in Cannon Street in the City of London.

At this time, I began my first manufacturing venture: a small steel tube factory. A machine which made spiral-welded pipes, then a relatively new and low cost method of production, was available. Because I could not afford to buy this equipment, I leased it. Huntingdon, one hour by train from London, seemed a convenient location and I was able to rent a building there. With £5,000 of borrowed capital and three workers, I started Natural Gas Tubes Limited. The steel coils used as raw material were bought on credit. It was tough going, made even harder by the intense scrutiny of the virtual monopolist in the steel tubes field. Stewart & Lloyds, a family business which was nationalized to become part of British Steel, dominated tube production in Britain. For reasons I still cannot understand, they became disturbed at my little activity and organized an annoying unofficial watch-and-probe effort. Eventually, convinced that NGT was no threat, they went away, but it was an uncomfortable experience.

Each day, I set out for Huntingdon with a lot of hope but not much cash. It was a living, but not a very gracious one. In 1968, our sales were £14,000. There were no great visions or extravagant hopes. I had no idea that this humble factory would become the wellspring of the future Caparo Group. I only had a conviction that things would turn out well if I worked hard and persisted.

Natural Gas Tubes was built on an opportunity. The late 1960s were years of shortage in the British steel industry. The producer was king, the customer was supplicant in a time of allocations and quotas. Consequently, manufacturers were not particularly interested in offering much customer service. I, however, was hungry and needed sales. It seemed to me that buyers would respond if I provided services which they did not receive elsewhere. My sales motto was: 'The right product with the right quality at the right time.' Our deliveries were prompt, shipments matched orders and quality control was carefully monitored. The reaction was most rewarding. I learned something which has been a guiding principle since then: if customers get the attention they need when their times are difficult, they will stay with you when your own times are difficult!

By the mid-1970s, NGT had expanded and was making steady profits. We were still a small business, but it soon was evident that we needed a new factory for our future. This would cost about £5 million. There was no way in which NGT or my personal assets could underwrite such capital outlays. We had to find other means to finance our growth. Fortunately, there were grants and soft loans available for industrial development in severely depressed regions of Britain. We began exploring those possibilities and locations which would qualify. A place which seemed suitable was South Wales, where unemployment was high and the economy was in extreme recession. It was also within reach of London, where I wished to continue living.

But another obstacle appeared. I was warned about the disposition of Welsh workers. They were reputed to be troublesome and truculent, an image which had kept investors away. I was told that it would be better to find another part of the country. At this stage, Michael Foot, a close and helpful friend, who was then Member of Parliament for the area, persuaded me to the contrary. He explained that Welsh labour would react well to fair leadership and the kind of extended family approach in which I believed. South Wales, he convincingly argued, was a good choice in human terms. With assistance from the British Department of Trade & Industry and the European Coal & Steel Community we were able to assemble a suitable financial package. Soon, construction was under way and a plant of 100,000 square feet was built. Its inauguration by the Prince of Wales in July 1977 gave us wide recognition. One year later, another new mill was added and declared open by Mrs Indira Gandhi.

There were still sceptics. We made a courtesy call on our major competitor, Stewart & Lloyds. Mindful that their parent, the giant state-owned British Steel Corporation, would be our principal raw material supplier, we politely asked whether they had any advice for small newcomers. The reply was quick: 'Pack up your machinery and send it back to America as soon as possible!' Despite this warning, we persevered, as we did in our relationship with British Steel, which today is excellent.

Currently, NGT (now Caparo Tubes) is one of Britain's leading manufacturers of welded steel tubes and spiral-welded pipes. It is the largest and most comprehensive of any UK cold formed steel producer. Factory space is now over 230,000 square feet, sales exceed £50 million annually and more than one-third of this is from exports. Never for an instant have I regretted moving to the so-called 'difficult' region of Wales. Our workers and the people of the locality have totally disproved the conventional wisdom of 1975.

During these years, other business interests evolved. They were subsumed under the acronym of Caparo, the name which was later to become the masthead of our group. We purchased the Osborne Hotel in the coastal resort of Torquay and the building which is now our group headquarters in Baker Street, London. Through takeover bids we acquired three British tea companies with extensive tea plantations in India. Caparo also engaged in shipping. This expansion was facilitated by the arrival of James Leek, then a young merchant banker, who joined Caparo in 1975. His presence doubled our senior staff! James was to continue as a key executive in our group for twenty years. An invaluable associate, his structured thinking meshed well with my own entrepreneurial approach. We worked closely together, planning and developing corporate strategy. Caparo was now ready for its second decade, a period bursting with challenges and the kind of stimulation which gives business its fascination.

Statistics cannot quite measure these excitements but, for the record, let me note that between 1978 and 1988 Caparo Group turnover increased from £4 million to £167 million.

To casual observers and to many in the financial community, the economic prospect looked dismal in 1979. Oil prices reached $40 per barrel. Interest rates were frightening and inflation was rising. There was considerable industrial unrest. Crude steel production in Britain had fallen from about 25 million tonnes in 1973 to below 10 million tonnes. Business confidence was very low—in the steel industry it had dived through the floorboards! Some suggested it was the precursor to another Great Depression. Yet, I felt this was a period of singular opportunity for those who took a long-term view. A decline in prices had brought once highly priced companies within Caparo's reach, and shareholders were prepared to consider offers which they would have ignored in better days. It was a moment for courageous action, if one had faith in the future of British industry. The dynamics of manufacturing, particularly in that segment of it called metal bashing—which refers to producers of steel-based consumable products for industry—were changing dramatically. Those who could transform the way in which companies were managed, who brought discipline and entrepreneurial skills to poorly organized enterprises, had a unique chance to improve profits and build value. It was a time for calculated risks, a rare time when buying companies and upgrading their facilities was cheaper, and could deliver a better return on capital, than erecting new facilities.

In 1981, Caparo embarked on a programme of acquisitions which brought us five significant domestic manufacturers by the end of the decade. All of them, except the smallest, were purchased through public takeover bids. The total cost was close to £150 million—paid in cash. Most of these new operations were assembled under the corporate banner of Caparo Industries Plc, a company listed on the London Stock Exchange. About 20 per cent of its shares were in the hands of outsiders. Caparo held the balance 80 per cent. Other parts of our activities belonged to a private company fully owned by me, the Caparo Group in total.

Our first acquisition was the CMT Industrial Group, purchased in 1981 for £14.5 million. CMT is a medium-sized diversified producer and distributor of pipe-fittings, insulation materials and specialized anti-vibration mounts. We had to compete against the mighty Hanson Trust for CMT. In retrospect, this was an encouraging experience because it proved that small but flexible entrepreneurs can still prevail in a world where size regularly triumphs. It also gave us the confidence to move ahead. Two years later, we bid for, and bought, the Barton Group for £9.6 million. Barton makes steel tubes and allied industrial items. In 1984, we negotiated another purchase, the Wrexham Wire Company, for £1.2 million. Wrexham then sold 13,000 tonnes of wire annually. It now sells over 56,000 tonnes and exports one-third of its output.

Some time later, in 1989, the Caparo Group made its largest domestic acquisition. The Armstrong companies cost £104 million. They are an engineering operation with worldwide sales of over £60 million, and are currently the biggest British makers of fasteners for the automobile industry. With Armstrong came two Spanish producers of components for the automotive industry. Caparo's first European plants, they are today a separate division with sales of around £22 million.

Buying companies is only one part of the game. Each business brings a distinctive ethos with it. Integration into the Caparo culture has not always been smooth and has required much adjustment. We have invariably made major capital investments and management changes, ruthlessly reducing overheads and cutting costs. Every operating unit must pay its way and there are no cross-subsidies in our group. This sometimes discomforts executives used to a more relaxed approach. Yet, the overall results have been gratifying, validating the Caparo dictum that there are few really bad businesses but many bad managements!

This, of course, is the pretty side of our picture. It even captivated us. By the mid-1980s we could do nothing wrong—or so we thought! Britain was in the midst of an economic recovery. Our acquisitions prospered, proving to be excellent investments. The financial press was highly favourable and financial institutions were supportive.

The shares of Caparo Industries were performing very well on the London Stock Exchange. I was proud of what we had achieved. Everything looked rosy. And then came Fidelity . . . For a while, our investment advisers, institutional shareholders and brokers had been proclaiming the need to shift the emphasis of our business. The argument went like this: Yes, Caparo had done well; it had created a profitable niche in the steel industry; it had proven management skills. But all this was only within the perimeters of sunset industries; metal fabrication was old fashioned—it was time to get into the sunrise categories. The days of hi-tech and consumerism had arrived. Our acknowledged talents would be a great asset when applied to the businesses of tomorrow. Why stick with the stodgy industrial sector when vast consumer markets were available? It was a plausible pitch.

Fidelity Plc, a well-known consumer electronics manufacturer based in north London, looked like the answer. This was one of the last surviving truly British producers of televisions, stereo systems and similar items. The company enjoyed good brand recognition. Although sales were stagnant and management was poorly regarded, the business apparently generated a net profit of £1.4 million in 1983. For Caparo, here was an attractive proposition. Surely, with better administration, income could be substantially increased.

Improved research and development would enable Fidelity to enhance its franchise. Perhaps, its technology might even support an entry into more sophisticated electronics. Potential possibilities included expansion into the huge new consumer markets which were awakening in India and other developing countries. Fidelity's shares were depressed, so we made an offer. Overcoming considerable opposition, we bought the company for £13.4 million.

When we took over management, it became clear that something was very wrong. Our investigations revealed glaring inaccuracies in stocks. Assets were much overstated. Goods in inventory were of unreliable quality. Questions received evasive answers. The true condition of the business was far worse than expected and elements of fraud surfaced. We acted immediately, instituting legal proceedings. There were three lawsuits. The first alleged fraud against former directors. After seven years, two key directors were found liable in the high court. This gave us little material satisfaction because the passage of time made any recovery of money impossible.

Our cases against Touche Ross, Fidelity's auditors, were also protracted. Caparo alleged negligence and asked for damages. Touche Ross responded that they had no responsibility to investors. Caparo lost in the lower court, but won at appeal. Touche Ross then challenged this judgement before the highest tribunal in the land—the House of Lords.

Although their challenge was sustained by the Lords, this case has provoked intense interest and is the source of much discussion in the accounting and commercial world. It has become a kind of landmark, unleashing deep concerns about the responsibilities of auditors, and may well bring about a redefinition of them. Subsequently, Fidelity itself initiated legal action against Touche Ross for negligence. This time they settled before trial by making a payment to us.

In the meantime, the operations of Fidelity were in deep trouble. To revive the company, we made major changes and introduced many efficiencies. In less than three years, overheads were reduced from £7 million to £5.5 million. The struggle for survival absorbed an enormous amount of Caparo effort. It may well have succeeded but for another disaster—market conditions deteriorated alarmingly. Fidelity's competition came entirely from imports made primarily in South Korea, Hong Kong, Taiwan and China. Trade with these companies was denominated in US dollars and, as this currency lost value, their products became cheaper. The decline of the dollar was ruinous. Fidelity was compelled to reduce prices by almost 20 per cent each year just to keep abreast of competition. The more we sold, the more we lost!

In our plight, there was no government protection or support. The Thatcher policy was to allow as much open trade as possible with the avowed objective of making British industry competitive in world markets. In many ways, this was a sensible approach, although a very painful one. However, there was a fatal flaw: the policy was strictly applied in Britain, but there was no way of ensuring that other countries played by the same rules. Fidelity's competitors could receive assistance from their governments while we had to make it on our own! We just could not do it. After four traumatic years we terminated the Fidelity operation. It was a serious loss for Caparo but an even greater loss for Britain: the field of consumer electronics was abandoned to foreign producers.

All was not gloomy in these times. In 1985, Caparo and British Steel joined in a venture which has been a happy endeavour. It came about in a rather casual way. At lunch with the British Steel Chairman, Sir

Robert Scholey, I offhandedly asked whether we could collaborate in any way. His equally nonchalant response was to mention a possible project in South Humberside. From this exchange came United Merchant Bar, a company 75 per cent owned by Caparo and 25 per cent by British Steel. Its background is this: British Steel had recently closed three small obsolete mills in the Humberside area. They wanted to begin a new plant in the locality, but there were restrictions imposed by the Department of Trade & Industry. They were, therefore, ready for a partner who would undertake the operation. Caparo was willing.

British Steel owned a disused rod mill in Scunthorpe. We virtually reconstructed a new facility on this site using the most advanced technology. As planned, UMB would produce 120,000 tonnes of merchant bar steel flats and angles, used primarily in the construction industry. But it was something more than another plant: UMB was a commitment to an industry which then seemed to have no future. At the opening ceremony in September 1986, the Chancellor of the Exchequer, Nigel Lawson, described it as 'a modern phoenix rising from the ashes of an outdated sector of Britain's steel industry'. He was right. UMB's performance has been outstanding. Production is now over 500,000 tonnes and about one-half is exported. It is among the world's most efficient producers, manufacturing high quality steel at low cost. Sales which were £9 million just ten years ago are now £72 million. The original capital input of £12 million is worth many times that amount. British

Steel, who have proved most cooperative partners, have received dividends far in excess of their investment. What has given me the most satisfaction is that UMB demonstrates the vitality of British industry, proving that state-owned corporations and the private sector can work harmoniously together to create a world-class enterprise in what was widely considered a dead-end business not so long ago!

Fresh horizons appeared in the late 1980s. I had long been intrigued by economic opportunities in America, a country I knew well but which had been outside my professional ambit. Suddenly, in a short period of five years, Caparo was able to establish a major presence in the United States. Our capital outlays there will soon reach $350 million and this has radically shifted the overall balance of our activities. Once again, unsuspected happenings have guided the destiny of Caparo. Much of our future will probably unfold in the western hemisphere, something unpredictable a few years ago. It is perhaps a closing of the circle. My exposure to modern technology began at MIT over four decades ago. As my corporate career moves towards its end, I am again drawn to this energetic society and its potential.

Our first American acquisition was Bull Moose Tubes in 1988. This was followed by Bock Industries in 1990. Both were well-known companies, each about thirty years old. Combined, they make Caparo the largest manufacturer of steel tubes in North America with current capacity exceeding 400,000 tonnes produced in five modern plants. The original cost of these businesses was $98 million, an amount much increased by improvements we have made in their facilities. The results have been extraordinary. Sales have more than doubled to around $200 million and profits have expanded from $9 million to over $20 million. This progress and the enthusiasm of our workers was the springboard for our next American venture.

Sharon Steel was an old and once well-regarded company, begun in 1900, which had collapsed into liquidation in the 1980s. Its large plant in Farrell, Pennsylvania was shut; its skilled labour force discharged. What remained of corporate assets was vested in bankruptcy court. The debacle at Sharon had wreaked havoc on surrounding localities. In late 1994, following a favourable article about Caparo in the prestigious financial periodical *Forbes*, I received a letter from the Pennsylvania Power & Light Company enquiring whether we would be interested in purchasing Sharon. Pennsylvania Power had lost a major customer with the demise of Sharon Steel and was anxious to revive this account.

My curiosity was aroused. We examined the steel mill and other facilities available. The state of Pennsylvania also indicated its commitment to economic regeneration of the region. We weighed the pros and cons. If we proceeded it would be Caparo's largest project, a major challenge drawing heavily on our financial resources and time. I decided to go ahead. A lot of preliminary groundwork was undertaken before we purchased the assets of Sharon for $26 million. Much more work and a further investment of $64 million was necessary to get production started. In June 1995, we formally reopened a plant with capacity of 1.2 million tonnes of hot rolled coil, 600,000 tonnes of cold rolled coil and 100 tonnes of galvanized sheets. At the entrance is a beautiful sculpture in memory of my daughter, Ambika.

An additional $180 million capital improvement and expansion programme is under way. For Caparo Steel, this has been a stimulating exercise, not least because it has helped to revive a dispirited community.

In 1991 we made an offer for the publicly owned shareholding of our subsidiary, Caparo Industries— 20 per cent of its total. This company had been listed on the London Stock Exchange for the preceding decade. Because the publicly held shares were so limited in number, taking Caparo Industries private was the best answer to a paradoxical situation: the stock market requires short-term results, while the engineering industry needs long-term investments whose real payback only comes after several years. Our subsequent growth validates this decision to offer a generous 50 per cent premium over the quoted price of 44p per share. Three thousand shareholders were very satisfied with the rewards for their confidence in Caparo, sentiments which were expressed at the special general meeting that approved our action. Managing a public company had been an enjoyable experience, but it was now time for a change.

Today, Caparo is a conglomerate of small- and medium-sized companies with total sales of over £500 million and operating profits in excess of £50 million in 1995. Our four thousand workers are a large family whose collective well-being depends on the effort of every single individual. The senior members of this family are our management.

I expect them to be entrepreneurs as well as executives, to take pride in what they do because they believe in it, not because they are paid well for a job. Within budgetary guidelines, Caparo managers have wide discretion to make about 90 per cent of the decisions which affect their companies, divisions or departments. They know that progress does not just mean increasing profits. It is in building an organization which is better than most of its competitors and building people who perform better than anyone in our industry. A few are born good managers, but most good managers have been created by hard work, focusing on objectives and accepting responsibility. In the modern business environment, the gifted amateur is more of a myth than a reality. It is professionalism, training and practicality which count.

Another critical ingredient in Caparo's approach is cultivating flexibility in our labour force. A visitor to any Caparo plant will see workers functioning with none of the usual job demarcations. Everyone is ready to undertake any assignment of which he or she is capable. This is easy to accomplish when starting a new operation; it is more complex when acquiring an ongoing industrial enterprise. Yet it is vital for competitiveness. We have been able to do so in both circumstances, sometimes after lengthy negotiations as happened on two recent occasions.

At Armstrong Fastenings, almost two years went by before we convinced skilled bolt machine setters to abandon a practice rigidly followed for several decades: they now set a whole bank of machines during a single shift instead of setting one machine and then taking time to observe its operation. This simple change, so difficult to secure, has enabled us to compete economically with Taiwan and Europe. Without it, we just could not! Similarly, at Bock Industries in Indiana, we introduced labour flexibility after twelve months of discussions with unions. A 4 per cent reduction in costs followed, saving over a million dollars annually!

The foundations of Caparo have been constructed on a central premise: we are makers of mass manufactured steel-based items used by other industries. These are often patronizingly called commodities. To me, they are attractive sources of profit. By continually improving production skills and being innovative in sourcing and pricing raw materials, we are able to compete in international markets. For the most part, I have prudently avoided operations involved in large, one-off capital goods or construction-type products. Make one mistake here, and all is lost! I have also generally shunned more fashionable consumer businesses. With personal taste increasingly fickle, these are too faddish and fanciful for my liking. My own style has been to search for companies and products that are suited to my temperament and outlook. I believe that anyone who engages in an occupation alien to his disposition will end in failure, sickness or unhappiness—and maybe all three! This is not my notion of a good life.

One important lesson I have learned concerns the use of technology in manufacturing. The most effective modern equipment may be expensive but, in the long run, is usually more economical. However, it must be *productive* equipment. Often, super hi-tech, state-of-the-art machinery can be too sophisticated for those who will be using it. I have obtained as good results by giving careful thought to machine layout, production, planning and improved logistics as by using advanced technology. The intelligent use of equipment is as important as the quality of the equipment itself. Equipment must serve the manager, not vice versa!

Here let me say a word about experts. Consultants, advisers and other specialists have become an ever-present escort for modern management. Their opinions and services are so frequently used that I wonder how many companies will survive without them. My own evaluation is less positive. Indeed, if I had listened to the experts, two of our most profitable ventures would not have begun. So, it is tempting to conclude that experts are worthless, although that is too extreme. Hear what they say but remember that advice is not a substitute for management decision making. The best business judgements are made not only on evidence available, but also with faith in how things might be—and imagination cannot be purchased by the hour! A sensitive and creative manager knows the limits of possibility in his organization. This is knowledge that is often intuitive. It can be realized, but can rarely be imparted.

Experience has taught me an allied lesson. We try to make our business decisions in the most logical manner. And it is right to do so. After all, where would society be if reasoned thinking did not exist? Yet, I have frequently found that logic alone, especially conventional logic, is not the best guide in decision making. Sometimes, there are constructs which carry a rationale of their own, and which ultimately prove more compelling than the most obviously sensible choices. This is frequently labelled as instinct, an indefinable quality that is incorrectly associated with impulse. I prefer to call it holistic analysis: assessments lodged as much in human, cultural and psychological impressions as in hard data or factual content. Business school analysts tend to discount these factors but, to me, they are vital elements which should not be ignored.

My businesses operate under very strict capital controls, what I like to call weight-loss programmes. Reduction of capital is another way of increasing profits. Income derived from a lower capital base has a higher value than the same income derived from a larger base. So, Caparo is constantly in a slimming struggle. Another part of this diet is the trimming of overheads. Like fat on the human body, overheads build up slowly, grow unnoticed, are difficult to shed and do a lot of damage. They easily become entitlements and perquisites which managements fight to preserve, often for prestige purposes. My policy is to cut overheads below what anyone thinks is possible. Let the cracks be repaired as they appear.

While this is not popular with executives, I have

rarely seen a bad business with too few overheads, or a good one with too many. In fact, one of the reasons why Caparo has been able to weather recessions is because our slogan for hard times is: 'Think lean, act mean, stay keen!'

To my mind, the key to corporate advancement is leadership. What is this type of leadership? It is both a commitment and a way of action. Contrary to textbook theory, there is no standard prescription or formula. There are, however, a few attributes which I think are useful yardsticks. A corporate leader does not have to be a visionary, yet he needs to have a vision. The vision may not always remain the same; it can change or evolve, but he must know where he wants to go at any time. He should clarify his objectives and focus on them relentlessly. A leader cannot afford too much distraction or relaxation. The company must come first, second and last. This does not mean neglect of family or leisure but recognition that the demands of the position require full attention: there is no such thing as a successful part-time leader! One of the principal tasks of the corporate chief is to balance the future with the present, the long-term with the short-term. He must be consistent in his application—it is all too easy to perform effectively and give preference to pleasant projects; the real test is whether a leader can do as well in less interesting or less fruitful endeavours.

A leader has to be decisive and demonstrate it— better a bad decision than no decision. He cannot be the captive of any policy or individual. He must have a lot of flexibility and no favouritism. The good captain is always ahead of his team because one can only lead from the front. Yet, to be too far ahead is to be out of touch or unable to motivate. It is the leader's responsibility to be sure that his staff know precisely what is expected of them. Lack of direction and confusion cause more management problems than almost any other lapses in leadership. Finally, a leader has to learn when to communicate and when to be discreet. Silence is sometimes a very good tool to deploy. In this context, there are two dangers against which eternal vigilance is required: feelings of omniscience and the traps of sycophancy. Nobody knows everything and those who think they do ignore the classical message that hubris precedes nemesis. Flatterers and toadies tend to cluster around leaders. Listen to them if you wish for entertainment, but never for fact. These are, of course, personalized perceptions which embody my own activist philosophy. The manners and methods of leadership vary vastly, but two basic truths are common: first, no enterprise has been successful without effective leadership; second, leaders *must* lead.

I have always considered work as a kind of religion, a faith and a way of life. Just as one respects religion, I believe one must respect work, and I am happiest when I am engaged in something which will make Caparo grow.

Expansion is the oxygen of business; to stand still is to fall behind. All this requires a lot of effort. There is really no magic formula. The secret *mantra* is work, work, work! It is true that a few get rich quick, but this is very rare luck. If you want to make a fast buck, you will generally do as well in a casino as in commerce!

In the end, business is about people. It is the most contact-driven economic activity in which human beings engage. Anyone who forgets this is in trouble. But human relations should not be confused with public relations. Customers, suppliers, workers and investors will ultimately judge you by sincerity rather than affability. It helps to have the latter, but it is essential to be the former. I have found this to be fundamentally true. In business life, there are ups and downs, and every outcome is not perfect. But there are few vocations which can give as much satisfaction and as good a living as a business career. I am convinced that it is possible, and not even unusual, for men and women of ideals to engage in business. It is an honourable profession when conducted by honourable people.

In early 1996, I handed over day-to-day operations of Caparo to my sons. Ambar and Akash are now Chief Executives of Caparo Industries and Angad is a Group Director. They have their own styles of management and their own plans for the future. This is as it must be. No father, no leader, can expect another generation to replicate the past. I will be sufficiently satisfied if they share the values which inspired me in the making of Caparo. As of now, I remain Chairman with a broad policy portfolio. This allows me the freedom to pursue wider interests while permitting participation in planning Caparo's future. It has been an exciting journey. The continuing prosperity and stability of Caparo will be the measure of my achievement.

6

Commitments and Values

In recent years, I have been surprised at the interest which so many people take in the lives of public personalities. Sometimes this borders on the prurient—and tabloid journalism flourishes. At other times, it reflects the natural curiosity which the average person feels about those who are constantly in the news. Often, especially with younger individuals, I believe it is a quest for identification with men and women and values that are admired. It surely tells us a lot about our society that so many seek role models in the modern media rather than among the traditional heroes, saints and other great figures of mythology.

Having received a certain amount of media attention during my career, I am frequently asked for details of how I live and what constitutes the motivation of my daily activities. In this chapter, I will try to respond to these questions and to explain the ideas which inspire my style of living. By contemporary criteria, I do not lead a very glamorous or flashy life. This may not be a very exciting section for those who look for glitzy tidbits.

I believe in a simple lifestyle. For thirty years, I have lived in essentially the same apartment—with a few modifications and enlargements to accommodate a growing family.

It is a roomy place because my wife and I feel that each person needs his or her own space. In recent times, it has become somewhat busy as our six grandchildren visit us so much. Yet, the pleasures of getting to know another generation quite offsets any loss of privacy. For those who value family associations, there is no greater reward than to see another cycle beginning.

Most of my life has evolved around my family and, in a very fundamental sense, I am a committed family man. When I was growing up, my parents and my siblings were my world. We shared everything. Today, as the extended family has become less popular, this way of living is considered stifling. However, the reinforcement, emotional support and security it provided was wonderful. Perhaps a certain individuality was sacrificed, but the values of unity and community were so encouraged that we developed a lifelong ethic of sharing. I think all this eventually contributes to a more cohesive society.

I married at the relatively young age of twenty-five. During the past forty-one years, my ever-caring

Aruna and I have tried to maintain the spirit of family togetherness. Of course, the circumstances of modern, urban dwelling necessitates adaptations.

Yet, to this day, we are a family that spends much time together—time that all of us enjoy—and these are my most relaxed moments. None of us—not even my twin sons—are identical in personality and emotions. But all of us feel some responsibility towards each other and cherish that feeling. I hope that in turn my grandchildren will also evolve these kinds of relationships.

Generally, I am a man of abstemious ways. I am a teetotaller, a vegetarian and do not smoke. This is not from any exaggerated sense of virtue or morality. It is just that I grew up in that manner and am comfortable with it. When I was young, these habits were somewhat abnormal in the western world. However, as time passes, a large number of people have become more health conscious and there is now no discomfort in adopting these customs. In matters of social taste and personal living, I do not think anyone should impose their beliefs on others—even on their children. It is better to be a model than a missionary. As Mahatma Gandhi said: 'Be yourself what you want to see in the world.' Those who agree with you will then follow your ideas out of conviction instead of doing so only to appear congenial.

Unless I am away from London, my daily routine does not vary much. I rise early to engage in a period of reflection. While not deeply religious in a formal sense, I believe that each individual should seek a relationship with the spiritual in the way that best suits him.

A more contemplative and introspective approach has always appealed to me. From our Hindu tradition comes this sentiment: 'The truth is one . . . men seek it in different ways.' And an ancient Greek philosopher once said that the unexamined life is not worth living. At a certain point, these two constructs intersect—and that is where I like to begin a meditation each day. Where we are and what we are, what we want to be and where we want to go . . . this, to me, is life's journey and we should look at our pathways as often as we can.

Inevitably, the early morning also brings many telephone calls from close friends and family. When these are disposed of, I go for a brisk walk in Regent's Park. Each Sunday, I extend this walk to London Zoo and to the Ambika Paul Children's Zoo and Memorial within it. I am not particularly ambitious by nature. Whatever advancement has come my way has been a consequence of hard work and not of predetermined aspirations. But, I do have one ambition these days and that is to maintain the Ambika Paul Children's Zoo as the best of its kind in the world. It is my own little tribute to my dear departed daughter.

After a light breakfast with Aruna, I go to my office in Baker Street. Since my sons are now fully responsible for the operations of Caparo, my workload is less than in years past. Nonetheless, there are many policy matters and other interests which require direction. This takes a large part of the morning.

Thereafter, whenever the House of Lords is in session, I attend daily. The House sometimes sits until evening, sometimes quite late, and I then go home for a family dinner. Aruna and I have a busy social life but we like to dine in our home as often as possible—and with as many of our extended family as we can gather.

It took me quite a while to become familiar with the procedures, the workings and the overall structure of the House of Lords. The House has its formalities, which begin each working day with the Lord Chancellor's procession and the commencement of proceedings. There is a question period, when the government has to reply to members' requests for information. This is followed by debates on legislation or other resolutions. As the senior chamber of the British legislature, the Lords has extensive parliamentary and judicial functions. For members who are regular attendees, a substantial amount of preparatory work needs to be undertaken. As I have become better acquainted with the character and the efforts of the House, I have come to appreciate the operations of the legislative process.

From my early years, I have been consistently involved in a variety of community activities and organizations. In modern society, individuals tend to be self-contained or feel that they have less time for voluntary social work.

This is unfortunate because the contemporary environment requires the enrichment that personal participation provides. Alienation and loneliness—the psychological characteristics of our age—might be much reduced if we could persuade more men and women to work with and for others. This is why I continue a number of voluntary efforts, especially trying to reach young people. Too many people of my age choose to associate almost exclusively with those of their own vintage and background. And, then, we express disappointment in the next generation!

Human relationships are among the most difficult of exchanges. Each of us is constrained by our circumstances, experiences and inhibitions. I have found interacting with others to be one of the most rewarding pursuits. Of course, it takes a lot of input— and I have been fortunately blessed with a somewhat outgoing personality. But I believe that everyone can try to communicate better and to be more understanding. In family, business and social life this makes for a remarkable improvement in the quality of personal relations. All the textbooks on how to get along with others can surely be reduced to three instructions: listen, reach out, show your concern!

A frequent question put to me is this: has wealth made any difference to your life? I can honestly answer that it has not changed me or my ways very much.

Perhaps this is because affluence came slowly, after a lot of hard work. I do take business risks, but they are carefully evaluated. In general, I do not gamble and do not speculate. Business is not a casino and a steady, long-term approach has served me well. This kind of attitude does not encourage conspicuous consumption. Comforts satisfy me, luxuries do not. So, I am happy if financial security makes life comfortable and I am not given to much more than that. The cultural tradition in which I was raised has a wonderful variety which embraces both extravagance and frugality. Each individual has the liberty to choose what is most suitable for him or her. To this, I would add another article of faith: Our heritage enjoins us to be what we are, to eschew pretensions and affectations. I have endeavoured to live my life this way—maybe not always with total success, but always to the best of my ability.

Where wealth has made a difference is in the opportunities which it has enabled me to provide for my children. I am deeply committed to education. It is a far better investment than any material asset. Financial resources can be dissipated; education cannot be lost. This is why I have urged all my children to obtain admission to the most advanced schools and universities in the fields they sought to enter. Thankfully, I was not disappointed. A substantial part of any success they have achieved is because of their education. Parents everywhere should regard education as the best legacy they can bestow on their children.

Education may or may not make character, but lack of education surely diminishes the perceptions and capacities that contribute to the building of character.

As I have seen the years pass, and my own circle of acquaintances has widened, I have given a great deal of thought to what is most important in an individual—what is it that matters most in life. My conclusion is: character. I would define this as a quality of inner strength founded on a sense of integrity and certain principles. Many of those whom

I admire have this core of faith in their values which then gives them faith in themselves. Ultimately, success in life does not come from cleverness or from money. Some of the most miserable people I know are very clever and very rich, and not all of them are very nice! Nor does professional success necessarily mean success in life. To my mind, success in life comes from the inner security which arises when an individual knows what he or she believes in is right and that every effort is being made to act accordingly.

Sometimes, our personal beliefs are not popular or very well received. And, then, it is quite easy to change them to suit prevailing opinion. Many people in public life do this quite often for whatever rewards they can obtain. It has always troubled me that so many trim their views in this way or are so reluctant to go against the mainstream.

A society that wants to sustain a high level of democracy needs to develop two characteristics—an environment in which individuals are able to dissent honourably without fear of punishment and an appreciation that democracy goes beyond politics into other areas such as corporate governance. Transparency, the openness surrounding decision making and the process leading to decision making, has recently been discovered and become a much used slogan. To me, it has always been a basic feature which underwrites the characteristics of democracy.

Almost twenty years ago, as I have discussed elsewhere in this book, I was engaged in a struggle for shareholder democracy with two of India's largest and most influential companies. Initially, I was motivated largely by business opportunity. It rapidly became obvious that vested interests were very concerned at my involvement. At first, I thought that their resentment was somewhat justified in a narrow-minded way—that they feared a loss of position or some dimunition of their so-called status. It was soon apparent that the essential cause of their frantic opposition was the fear that corporate malfeasance would be exposed. I had no idea, until I got well into these situations, that corporate governance was in such need of cleansing and that transparency was then almost unknown at the highest levels of the corporate ladder.

This was the real reason for the pressures and other attacks upon me. Among the strategies used was to get important individuals to try to change my mind. When I once confronted a principal in one of the companies about the use of company funds for personal purposes, his reply was: 'Swraj, why are you worried? Everybody does it.' But I knew I was right and the support I received from the public, small shareholders and many in the media confirmed this. In fact, one eminent journalist told me: 'If so many self-styled tycoons are against you, you must be doing something honest!'

When the Escorts–DCM controversy was over, I felt a deep obligation to continue a public discussion about corporate malpractices. The reaction of small investors to my efforts and their positive response to my message encouraged me. For almost two decades, I have tried to use every possible forum to speak out about the need for management accountability in developing economies, especially India. My family often feels I have overstretched myself—accepting speaking, media and other invitations to pursue this debate. Indeed, several of my friends joked that I had made this a kind of mission or crusade! My own feeling is that when one is convinced one must do whatever possible in whichever way is most effective—especially if there are few others who can do so.

There have been four overall themes to my argument. First, corporate malpractice in public companies takes away the patrimony of the people, particularly in poorer countries. Where such ways are widespread, it is difficult for capital markets to evolve properly and the development of nations is retarded. Last year, the crisis in Southeast Asia subsequently proved this point very dramatically. As these processes unfold, the small investor is deprived of his savings. Second, for effective development of countries like India, it is essential to draw these smaller investors into the equities markets. For enterprise to play its full role in the national development it has to harness the support of smaller investors—not devour them. This broadbased participation is the best way of underwriting economic progress and political stability.

My third point concerns how to assure proper business practices. There are two ways in which to do this. Corporate leaders should set examples. Transparency is an absolute necessity in order that knowledge is available. And transparency can only be enforced by government insistence on appropriate procedures and regulations. I believe that governments should have little direct involvement in ownership or management of business. But governments do have a responsibility to see that the corporate sector operates properly and within the law.

Finally, I have argued in many forums that economically developed countries have responsibilities too. By this, I mean that when businessmen from the advanced industrial countries succumb to temptations or irregularities in other parts of the world they become accessories to malpractice. Speaking in the House of Lords in a debate concerning India's fifty years of independence in October 1997, I emphasized the current relevance of this:

> Let me add a word on an issue of particular importance in current commercial transactions with the subcontinent and elsewhere. Let us export all we can of value and values, but we must not encourage abroad malpractices we deprecate at home. We must avoid contributing to the debasement of business ethics and standards. The OECD has now publicly expressed its concern about such matters. The Foreign Secretary, too, has commendably endorsed an ethical approach in his mission statement.

When I first began focusing on this external facilitation of malpractice only the United States had enacted legislation—the Foreign Corrupt Practices Act of 1977—and that, too, was not very effective. Since then, the World Bank, the Organization of Economic Cooperation and Development, and several industrial states have begun to realize its corrosive nature. In November 1997, the twenty-nine member-countries of the OECD drafted a treaty which addressed this concern.

It is not a very strong agreement and will be operative only after 1998. But it is a signal that the issue of transnational malpractice is becoming more significant on the international agenda. This is only a start and I am sure that the momentum for strong action will gather in the years ahead. Those of us who have fought this battle from its earliest days cannot afford to now relax our efforts.

Activities such as this, together with my work at Caparo, have left little time for recreation. Recently, however, my sons have assumed executive management of our business and so I expect my corporate tasks will reduce. I hope it will be possible to pursue my often postponed desire to do more reading of traditional scriptures and writing. From what little I know, I have been amazed at the wisdom of the ancients and their insights. Cross-cultural experiences have always interested me—and have also proven very useful in international business operations. I would like, for instance, to undertake a comparative study of the Mahabharata, our magisterial Indian epic, with some similar Western literature like Homer's stories of heroes past. I do not profess intellectual prowess in these areas, but I do believe that, as we get older, we must try to do more of what we want to do.

Younger people need to be encouraged to accept and discharge responsibility. In the area of corporate governance, in India and abroad, they will have to continue the mission to cleanse the environment. It is only persistent struggle that will diminish what has become a kind of disease in many countries—and it is a sickness that will destroy democracy where it exists or sustain authoritarianism elsewhere. At the heart of it all is an unholy nexus between politics and business. If this can be cleansed, the quality of public life will improve immeasurably. If not, we will see a deterioration of society that will engender frustration and violence. The task for young people, particularly in developing regions, is to build on the early and only partially successful efforts that many of us have initiated. In my own way, I hope I have been able to convey these values to them. I have certainly tried for quite a while.

Some twenty centuries ago, the Roman statesman Cicero listed the six primary mistakes in life. Let me summarize them:

— the delusion that personal gain is made by demeaning or crushing others
— the tendency to worry too much about things we cannot control
— insisting that something is impossible because we cannot accomplish it
— refusing to put aside trivial preferences
— neglecting cultivation of the mind
— attempting to compel others to believe and live as we do

Long ago, when I first read this, I resolved to make it a kind of credo to build into my lifeways. I have not been able to accomplish this fully. Men and women who have led very busy lives will understand how the best of intentions do not always get fulfilled. But, in the future, I will try harder, for I believe that effort and learning have to be lifelong.

7

Indira Gandhi

Indians of my generation virtually grew up with Indira Gandhi. She was a constant public presence as a daughter of the Freedom Movement; then as a prominent young political and social activist; finally, as a national leader and Prime Minister in 1966–77 and again in 1980–84. She provoked strong emotions. Many liked and many disliked Indira Gandhi. Few were neutral about her. As probably the most important woman of our century, Mrs Gandhi attracted enormous attention. Writings about her range from serious studies to hate diatribes, all in ample numbers. I cannot claim the expertise or skills required for such efforts. To me, Indira Gandhi was a friend, almost an elder sister, and a person who deeply influenced my life. My recollections are consequently more personal and probably more favourable than those of most others.

My original direct contact with Mrs Gandhi was through her political associate and Cabinet Minister L.N. Mishra, an earthy and energetic leader from Bihar. Mishra and I had become close friends since we first met in the late 1960s. Although reputed to be a master politician and fund-raiser, I found Mishra to be forthright and loyal. He was a man of his word, without any of the pretensions which usually attend notables from South Asia. We spent many pleasant and amusing moments together whenever I visited India or he went abroad.

Often he would ask me to accompany him on his official journeys, much to the chagrin of Indian bureaucrats who believe that they should monopolize the attention of any Indian dignitary, regardless or his or her preferences. I experienced this when going with Mishra to the United Nations Conference on Trade & Development (UNCTAD) in Santiago, Chile in 1972, and also in travelling with Mrs Gandhi when she was Prime Minister. Mishra was a shrewd, grass-roots oriented adviser. His assassination in January 1975 deprived Mrs Gandhi of wise counsel which might have prevented some of the problems which afflicted her thereafter.

In 1971, Mishra was visiting Britain and so was Mrs Gandhi. He introduced me to her personal assistant, R.K. Dhawan, who arranged an appointment. Dhawan, a close friend in later years, was infinitely devoted to Mrs Gandhi. He requested me to call at Claridges Hotel where the Prime Minister was staying. This, my first one-to-one meeting with Indira Gandhi, was a memorable occasion, but more for the impression it made on me than for the substance of our discussion. Mrs Gandhi was preoccupied with the Bangladesh crisis. She was deeply disturbed about its possible effect on India and was singularly unhappy at the lack of support from major Western countries.

At this time, the positive attitude of the Soviet Union made a difference, earning that country the prolonged goodwill of India. It was an opportunity missed by the West, an opportunity which would have cost nothing because the outcome was inevitable, whatever they did or did not do. Mrs Gandhi knew that I had, for several months past, been vigorously engaged in writing to the press and contacting opinion makers in support of India's position. The moments she gave me, and the thoughts she shared, were her way of saying 'thank you'.

Two things especially impressed me about Mrs Gandhi. She seemed to have a deep and sincere interest in overseas Indian communities and in ways of drawing them closer to their motherland. A decade later, this interest was to have fateful consequences for me. Even more interesting than this was her capacity to maximize the use of time in interpersonal relations—when she wanted to. Each meeting that I had with her, however brief, left me with a strangely satisfying sensation that I had said everything I wanted to say, so complete and focused was her attention. I never came away feeling there was anything left unsaid. This was an attribute that many have noted: a short interview seemed so much longer than it actually was. Too many leaders are either brusque because they are under pressures of schedule, or get so enthused by the sound of their own voices that a meeting becomes an endless monologue.

Mrs Gandhi must have found my visit congenial because she asked me to see her whenever I came to India. This I did on several occasions in the next few years. She was always the most courteous of hosts. Our conversations were of a rather general nature but I was becoming increasingly aware of her extensive knowledge and incisive grasp of affairs. She wanted to know what the world was thinking of India and was particularly inquisitive about the attitudes of ordinary people. It was clear to me that she was not very happy with official reports and valued an objective analysis, even if it was unpleasing. This interest was so intense that I often felt like a sounding board, an extension of her eyes and ears abroad! As I got to know Mrs Gandhi better, I began to appreciate the essential duality of her person: how her gracious personal style contrasted with her stern public image. Later on, I had more occasions on which to observe her extraordinary capacity to put anyone in her company at ease, and her ability to make the atmosphere unbearably uncomfortable for those who did not particularly engage her—both without word or sign!

In 1973, I first gained some insight into the aura of intrigue which infused the circle of associates around Indira Gandhi. At this time, her younger son, Sanjay, had begun his initial business venture—an automobile assembly project—which was the subject of much criticism. On a trip to Delhi I was asked by Mishra to look at Sanjay's plant and assess whether it was viable.

I visited the location and had my first meeting with Sanjay. He was pleasant but somewhat laconic, an inherent trait that was not to fit well in the excessively talkative ethos of Indian politics! His project seemed workable. It was a relatively unsophisticated operation—the assembly of parts manufactured elsewhere into a low-priced 'people's car'. There were a few potential costing questions but my overall observations were favourable. Mishra conveyed these conclusions to Mrs Gandhi, who used them in her refutation of attacks on Sanjay's venture. It was then that I came to know that the real source of many of these attacks was not her political opponents—they were only the mouthpieces—but individuals in her own office. At one and the same time, they were working for Mrs Gandhi and also against her, facts of which she was not unaware. It still puzzles me why she tolerated this kind of infighting among those around her. Was it some manipulative streak of character or was she merely accepting the conventional behaviour of courtiers who surround great centres of power in traditional societies?

Two years later, in 1975, Mrs Gandhi was under siege. The afterglow of the successes of 1971, the stunning victory over Pakistan followed by an election triumph, had faded. The political opposition had united under the patriarchal Jayaprakash Narayan who now called for 'total revolution'. The crisis suddenly escalated when a law court in Allahabad delivered an unfavourable judgement against Mrs Gandhi in a case about violations of election rules which had taken place four years earlier.

According to the verdict, which was instantly appealed, she could not now hold public office. I recalled L.N. Mishra's last words to me. Two days before he was killed, a few months earlier, Mishra had said: 'Swraj, certain people are bent on destabilizing this government because they cannot beat it by the ballot box. They are using me as their first line of attack and their next line will be Mrs Gandhi.' The Prime Minister was in serious trouble. I felt deeply for her and was very worried about the situation in India. Given the prevailing turbulence in the country and the region, her departure from office would be a disaster. After all her efforts, was this not an unmerited humiliation? Impulsively, I flew to Delhi. There was nothing I could do, but I wanted to assure Mrs Gandhi of my support and urge her not to yield to the pressures which were crowding in. It was a gesture of which she was most appreciative.

India was on the brink of chaos. Mrs Gandhi's response to the rising turmoil was to declare a State of Emergency. This was not her idea alone: several chief ministers of Indian states and several cabinet ministers ardently advocated it. Some of them have since pretended their innocence. The Emergency was approved by both the President and the Parliament of India. From June 1975 to March 1977, the country was governed in a quasi-authoritarian way. This was always intended to be a temporary measure and, at first, was widely popular. Order was restored, the economy began to show solid gains, a sense of national discipline was evident.

Gradually, however, two negative features began

to emerge. A small group of self-seeking politicians and officials began to cluster around Sanjay Gandhi, feeding this inexperienced man with grandiose ideas about transforming the nation. The problem with situations such as the Emergency is that fanciful notions can be transformed into policies. Sanjay embarked enthusiastically on what were essentially worthy projects, like population control and slum clearance. But this enthusiasm was crude and heavy-handed. Those around him heartily applauded his actions, while concealing the depth of their unpopularity. A parallel government was emerging with Sanjay at its centre. The culture of sycophancy, so much part of Indian society, is perhaps as much to blame as Sanjay himself.

A second problem was lodged in Mrs Gandhi's own political behaviour. The Emergency was the one time when she lost touch with the grass roots of politics. Throughout her life, Mrs Gandhi was remarkably sensitive to two wellsprings of opinion— to, as she put it, the masses and the chattering classes. She was always conscious of public reaction and sought innumerable ways of getting feedback from ordinary people. Although she was less swayed by the attitudes of intellectuals and the press, she also understood their concerns very well and was alert to them. The totality of the Emergency closed off both avenues of awareness. She was disconnected from her mass constituency, and a censored media published only the most praiseful news.

As a result, she became the victim of the worst kind of communications blockade—abuses began to take place of which she had no knowledge and the informal information reaching her was so exaggerated that it was easily dismissed as proveable propaganda. Without a free press, India became a land of rumour and wild speculation, almost all of it anti-government. Since much of this was also anti-Sanjay, Mrs Gandhi increasingly became a defensive and ill-informed mother protecting a helpful son from unjustified attack!

Yet, I remember how ambivalent Mrs Gandhi was about the Emergency. She was always asking about the way the British press was portraying it and how people abroad were reacting. Above all, it was clear to me that she, the daughter of Jawaharlal Nehru, and a believer in representative government herself, did not want history to regard her as the destroyer of Indian democracy. She was also uncomfortable with the way in which some of her lieutenants were throwing their weight around. When Om Mehta, the Minister of State for Home Affairs and a key figure in enforcing the Emergency, visited London I appealed to him against the impounding of some passports of Indian citizens living in Britain. Mehta haughtily replied: 'These people are against India.' I said that they were anti-Indira but certainly not anti-India, to which Mehta answered, 'It's the same thing!' Nothing I said made him see reason, so I told him that if this was the government's view of the value of an Indian passport, they could have mine back right away.

That very day I applied for a British passport. A few months later, when I reported this incident to Mrs Gandhi, her comment was: 'Why do you listen to this nonsense? It is things like this that are killing my name. I don't know why these people behave like this.'

In fact, the Emergency was neither as bad as its opponents described, nor as glorious as the official media proclaimed. It stands as a warning to the ease with which leaders can become isolated. This is as true of business as it is of politics. Those who hold positions of power are prime candidates for self-delusion. All they are told, and all they see around them, appears to confirm their own wishful convictions. Associates are too frightened or too anxious for advancement to tell the truth. Things filter through the most roseate lenses. One of the most important responsibilities of modern leadership is to find ways of keeping lines of feedback open. It is also self-preservation insurance! This was a lesson Mrs Gandhi never again forgot.

Living in London and closely following the international media, I was profoundly troubled. A great deal of misinformation was being disseminated, and the government's case was losing by default. In late 1975, I decided that something should be done to give the Indian government's position an open hearing.

Mrs Gandhi agreed and decided to send the President of her political party, D.K. Barooah, and a Cabinet minister, D.P. Chattopadhyay, for a series of meetings I would organize in London. The naysayers went into action at once and tried to sabotage my efforts.

The centrepiece of the Barooah–Chattopadhyay

visit was a large dinner which I was hosting at the Hilton Hotel. Over four hundred distinguished guests, opinion makers and prominent public figures had accepted my invitation. There were representatives and speakers from both the Labour and Conservative parties. The naysayers sent out a sheaf of letters requesting the better-known invitees not to attend and did everything they could to prevent the departure of the two delegates from India. Nothing worked and the programme went ahead as planned. The dinner was a splendid occasion at which British Cabinet Minister Michael Foot and Conservative shadow foreign secretary Reginald Maudling spoke. Everything went well, except that Barooah's exceptionally long address was rather tedious. Used to the verbal tempo of Indian public life, he refused to heed any advice and proceeded on the principle that the more you say the more convincing you are! Anyway, Mrs Gandhi was pleased at the exposure which her representatives received and that her side of the story was told.

Helping me with these arrangements was Eldon Griffiths, a Member of Parliament and an aficionado of India. We were so encouraged by the response to our efforts that we decided to institutionalize them. The Indo-British Association was born. For almost twenty years, the association kept the flag of India aloft in Britain. We had many social and cultural programmes, all of which were well attended. Here, I must acknowledge the energetic input which Griffiths, a warm friend, brought to the IBA. The high point of our activities took place on 22 March 1982 when our annual dinner was attended by two prime ministers— Mrs Indira Gandhi and Mrs Margaret Thatcher. It was a rare occasion when political ideologies took a back seat and the spirit of friendship between Britain and India was touchingly evident. In my remarks, I drew attention to the unique nature of this cordiality. Only thirty-five years after the end of colonialism, ruler and ruled had a better relationship than ever before. It has taken other countries much longer to reconcile to the end of imperial domination: thirty-five years after the American War of Independence, Britain and the United States were again at war!

The Emergency inevitably moved to its close. In March 1977, Mrs Gandhi called a general election. It was a free and fair event. Rarely have leaders with such power and state resources at their command held this type of truly democratic poll and unquestioningly accepted a negative verdict.

I visited Mrs Gandhi only once during the campaign. She was beginning to feel that an antagonistic tide was flowing. Back in England, I anxiously awaited the result. On 20 March, I spoke with her by telephone. She said: 'Yes, we are losing.' It seemed as if she was quite reconciled to the verdict of the people. Two days later she resigned. In some ways, the end seemed to come as a relief.

I was in touch with her quite often in those post-election days. Mrs Gandhi told me that she was now free to do things she had missed. She would, at last, see more of her grandchildren, spend much more time with her family and friends, do more reading, and go to Kashmir—a part of the country she loved. I invited her to visit Britain and she thought this would be a good break: 'Just give me a room in your flat and we will go to the bookshops and take it easy for a while.' Had the Janata government, now in office, gone about its business properly, I am confident that Indira Gandhi would have retired into a more relaxed life and receded into the political background. She would never have been inactive—she was sixty years old and full of energy. But her wide range of activities, most of which were non-political, would have absorbed her; and her interest in foreign countries and cultures would surely have taken her abroad frequently.

This peaceful scenario was not to be. The Janata government was more interested in persecuting Mrs Gandhi and Sanjay than in administering the country. A never-ending tirade of inquiries, charges, harassments and humiliations was heaped upon them. Betrayals were hard to bear. Several of her former ministers—supplicants at her feet for years—began to publicly testify against her in a shameless display of cowardice and an attempt to secure the favour of those now in power. Investigation after investigation, inquiry after inquiry proved fruitless. The vengeance and frustration of the government was boundless. Mrs Gandhi and her son were both imprisoned for brief periods. They had to be released because there was no sustainable evidence and public outrage was high. Eventually, Mrs Gandhi's so-called misdeeds of the past were projected as an excuse for Janata incompetence and misgovernment.

The stream of vilification was also directed at those who had helped Mrs Gandhi in any way. My brother Jit was accused of having improperly loaned a few jeeps to the Congress Party for election use in 1977. Attempts were made to induce him to say that our firm, Apeejay, had been coerced into providing these vehicles. Since almost every business house in India assists political parties during campaigns, there was nothing unusual or exceptional in Jit's actions. Nonetheless, he was under intense pressure to give false testimony—which, of course, he refused to do. Although it all ended in a fiasco, it was a frightening experience.

The agents of the Janata government made numerous attempts to disturb me in London. One of the reasons for this was a belief that Mrs Gandhi had vast sums of illegal funds stashed abroad and I was the custodian. Versions of this rumour have circulated occasionally in India. The truth was quite the contrary. Not only did Mrs Gandhi have no money abroad, she required little for her abstemious lifestyle. Her habits and tastes were inexpensive. Some of India's recent leaders have used power to get money; some have used money to get power. Mrs Gandhi did neither. My knowledge of her suggested that she was not much concerned with monetary matters. Her own attitude to wealth was typical of old-style patricians: she was detached from it and looked upon commercial transactions as rather sordid. There was no material greed in her. This is the reason why all the attempts to unearth Mrs Gandhi's so-called fortune have failed. There wasn't any! She died, as she had lived, a woman of modest means.

The Janata attempts to implicate me amounted to nothing. They were more annoying than damaging. Yet, they showed the extent to which Janata venom would go. In 1977 I met Atal Bihari Vajpayee, the Janata Foreign Minister and one of the few balanced leaders of the regime, in London. I told Vajpayee that, come what may, I remained an ardent supporter of Mrs Gandhi. His reply: 'I am glad to find an admirer of Mrs Gandhi; it has become a rare thing in India.'

The larger tragedy of the Janata was this: they missed an opportunity to establish a reputable two-party system in India. Democracies need stable alternatives. The Janata consisted of many experienced political leaders but their actions were so childish and mean-spirited that they discredited themselves, did no good to India, and failed to serve Indian democracy when it was well within their grasp to do so.

All their calumny and revenge created its own backlash. It aroused Mrs Gandhi to new levels of resolve, as much to protect her son as to restore her political fortunes. She was determined to fight this victimization and realized that it had to be done politically since the judicial process had been circumvented by creating special commissions and the like. As she once put it, justice had to be fought for in the streets because it was so hard to get elsewhere! Her political party had been hijacked by some erstwhile ministers who were keen on toadying to the new government. So, Mrs Gandhi formed a new party which instantly gained much popularity.

Her esteem among the masses began to return. Tired of Janata ineptitude and disgusted at their treatment of the former Prime Minister, ordinary people rallied to her call. In November 1978, Mrs Gandhi contested a by-election and was returned to Parliament with a resounding majority. She was now set for a comeback.

During the three years of the Janata government, I was advised not to visit India. Even so, I had kept in close touch with Mrs Gandhi and continued to argue her case at every opportunity. I had invited Mrs Gandhi to Britain on several occasions. Finally, just after her by-election victory, she accepted and scheduled her first foreign journey after losing office. As preparations for Mrs Gandhi's trip took place, all sorts of difficulties were created. It was obvious that the Janata government and its supporters abroad were fearful of the exposure and impact Mrs Gandhi's visit would have. As her programme evolved, attempts were made to abort it. The Janata government signified its displeasure through official channels; the Indian High Commission in London raised as many hurdles as possible; segments of the Indian community were mobilized to protest; a negative media campaign was launched. Some journalists even objected to Mrs Gandhi being allowed to enter Britain. Others advised British public figures not to meet her, or to stay away from events which she would attend. I decided to meet every obstacle head-on. And this, with Eldon Griffiths's aid, I was able to do.

Mrs Gandhi, accompanied by her daughter-in-law Sonia, landed at London's Heathrow Airport on 12 November. Ten hectic days followed. The visit created tremendous interest and was headline news. No political leader out of office has got such attention in Britain. On the night of her arrival, Mrs Gandhi dined at my house. Her informality and charm engaged us all.

The next day, Mrs Gandhi addressed an assembly of British Members of Parliament in one of the large committee rooms of the House of Commons. We were told to anticipate a hostile audience. Over one hundred MPs were present. Mrs Gandhi said a few words and questions followed. I braced myself for the storm, and it came with the first question: 'Mrs Gandhi, what went wrong with your Emergency?' Her response was simple and direct: 'We managed to upset nearly every section of the community simultaneously.' This remark caused a gust of laughter and the tense atmosphere dissolved. Everything went off smoothly after that.

But it was not all easy going. The media was determined to ask her the most trying questions and they did. Her skilful answers and gracious manner defused much of their hostility. One reporter shouted: 'Are you trying to make a comeback?' Her smiling retort: 'But where have I gone?' Jonathan Dimbleby, the celebrated telejournalist, recorded a searching interview with her, full of pointed questions and sharp queries. After it was over, he explained that it was not any personal antagonism which provoked this attitude but the intense curiosity of his television audience. Mrs Gandhi's comment was: 'That's all right and it is your duty to do so. Interviews abroad are entertainment for me. My electorate is in India!'

How things have changed! Today, no foreign television appearance by any leader goes unseen or unnoticed back home.

A memorable moment was Mrs Gandhi's visit to Southall, a suburb of London heavily populated by Asians. At the request of the Indian Overseas Congress she was invited to speak at a public gathering. We were informed that a group of troublemakers would disrupt the event. The organizers asked whether she would prefer to cancel it. Mrs Gandhi's response was that she did not want her meetings to be cancelled by anyone! The Southall function was attended by over 4,000 people of Indian origin who had come from all over the country. The tumult was extraordinary; there was shouting, cheering, abuse and applause. Some shrieked that Indira killed democracy. Despite the disturbances, Mrs Gandhi was able to make a short statement to huge acclaim. She observed afterwards: 'What sort of democracy do these people want? They don't want others to speak.'

The Indo-British Association held a large dinner in honour of Mrs Gandhi. The manoeuvres behind the scenes were almost more interesting than the formal programme. Mrs Gandhi's opponents did all they could to upset the arrangements. Important guests were pressured to avoid or evade the evening. A prominent columnist even demanded that the British Cabinet Minister and Opposition leaders scheduled to speak desist from doing so. Lord Mountbatten, last Viceroy of India and close friend of the Nehru family, refused to attend although he invited Mrs Gandhi for tea at his residence.

Tremendous efforts were made to prevent the Indian High Commissioner, N.G. Goray, from coming. And so it went on. In the end, it all worked out well. Michael Foot and Peter Shore, members of the Cabinet, were present and spoke eloquently. Lord Carrington, Conservative Party Leader in the House of Lords, also addressed the guests. Even High Commissioner Goray, rejecting the advice of his officials, was present. It was a splendid personal tribute to Mrs Gandhi, made more meaningful because she had no official position and there was such an orchestrated effort to undermine the meeting.

An interesting sequel arose from this function. About a month after her trip, an Indian news magazine maliciously reported that, while the evening proceeded, Mrs Gandhi had made some disparaging remarks about me to Sonia in French. This was, of course, ridiculous because Mrs Gandhi did not speak a word of French during the evening. Yet, she was much distressed by this press item and wrote me a moving letter, parts of which I reproduce below:

> I have very pleasant memories of my stay in London. I fully realise how much you contributed to its success. Sonia and I were both charmed by your family. In fact, Sonia repeatedly told me how unlike you were to the normal description of an industrialist.
>
> I very rarely go out, but the other evening I went to a small dinner with one of Rajiv's pilot friends, whose father-in-law is with the World Bank in New York. I was horrified to hear from one of the guests that I had made rude remarks about you

to Sonia while you were in the room. This ridiculous item has appeared in the 1st January issue of *India Today* magazine. Needless to say, there is not an iota of truth in this. It is not in my nature to make catty remarks either in the presence or behind the backs of people. At your dinner, after our arrival, I did not come anywhere near Sonia, except when we were leaving, and I certainly made no remarks about you. I was a little worried about her, as normally she avoids any such function, and you know how very reluctant she was to attend. However, afterwards she said that she had enjoyed it mainly because she was sitting by your family.

With good wishes to you and the family.

Yours sincerely
Indira Gandhi

The visit was a singular success in other ways. Mrs Gandhi met numbers of important individuals and gave innumerable interviews. Although the Foreign Office had reservations, she was invited to Downing Street to talk with Prime Minister James Callaghan. She met the Leader of the Opposition, Margaret Thatcher, and had a cordial discussion. We flew by helicopter to Wales, where Mrs Gandhi opened an extension of my steel factory and charmed her Welsh listeners with a graceful speech.

Whenever she appeared in public, large numbers of men and women came to see her in a friendly and admiring way. She was visibly touched by a group of young Indian girls who came to Claridges Hotel to sing on her sixty-first birthday. After the rough passage of the past two years, it was, as Mrs Gandhi put it, 'like a dream'.

On her arrival, Mrs Gandhi was somewhat apprehensive about her reception. Today, it is difficult to imagine the hostility which then existed. The Emergency had left a terrible image and the sustained worldwide campaign against its author had blackened her reputation beyond belief. Things began to change with her visit, a change that was to be complete with her massive election victory a year later. During her ten days in Britain, I observed the return of Mrs Gandhi's self-assurance. Encouraged by the welcome she received, there was a palpable transformation in her mood. Once again, she was on top of things and whatever slights occurred were taken in her stride. On her return journey, when she passed through Moscow, the Soviet leader, Leonid Brezhnev, cleverly sidestepped a meeting. At this, she amusedly remarked: 'The next time they will come calling.'

I got to know Mrs Gandhi well on this visit. I saw how considerate she was of other people, how she disliked inconveniencing anyone around. Her essential simplicity was unexpected and it was astonishing to see the almost girlish delight she took in opportunities for informal relaxation—a private meal in an unknown restaurant, an unguarded walk on the street, a casual visit to a bookshop, an unplanned visit to the theatre. I realized how much she had personally sacrificed for political life. There obviously are satisfying compensations in public life, and I have no doubt that Mrs Gandhi enjoyed them. But there was a deeper side to her personality which cherished so many of the things which leaders cannot do, and seemed to yearn for them. That this took some toll on her I am sure; how much and in what ways, nobody can tell. In any event, Mrs Gandhi was very happy with the outcome of her visit.

12 Willingdon Cresent
New Delhi
20.11.78

Dear Mr Paul,

I hardly have the words to thank you for all the trouble you took over my programme. But for your personal interest and constant vigilance the visit would not have been a success. I should like to thank your wife for her hospitality. The first evening at your home was a delightful and relaxing beginning to what turned to be a most hectic schedule. I was charmed by your children. You should really be proud of them.

I am sending you this small gift, typically Indian, to remind you of us.

With every good wish

Sincerely
Indira Gandhi

Back in India, the political winds were blowing in her favour. But there were still many difficulties to be faced. In early 1979, Mrs Gandhi wrote to me from Delhi:

You cannot imagine the mad rush we are in just now. The Government and the Janata Party are doing their worst, stepping up their harassment, changing officials, especially at the lowest levels and passing laws which are highly discriminatory. The usual rumour-mongering and spreading of false stories is again increasing. However, the people are with us. I am sure that in spite of anything that may happen they will prevail—so don't be depressed!

By the end of the year, elections were again under way. The campaign was the hardest she had fought. In seven weeks, Indira Gandhi trekked 52,000 miles across the country, made over 700 speeches and was estimated to have been personally seen by over 200 million Indians. Her popularity was higher than ever. I returned to India on Christmas Day 1979 and had lunch with the Gandhi family. It was good to see how cheerful and upbeat they were.

The election was a landslide for Indira Gandhi. Her son, Sanjay, was also vindicated by his own handsome victory in a parliamentary constituency. In the last days before the polls, I saw the tremendous hopes and expectations which simple voters had. Mrs Gandhi was to be their saviour.

They believed that a new age was dawning, that her leadership would bring an era of order, prosperity and peaceful progress. I did, too. We were to be disappointed, as Mrs Gandhi herself was to be. I believe the last four years of her life were more difficult and painful than could be conceived. In that time, I do not think Indira Gandhi had much peace of mind or happiness.

That, however, was in the future. As I took leave of her in January 1980, it was euphoria all the way. Huge crowds surged round her residence at Willingdon Crescent. Her opponents were crushed. Those who betrayed her now sought to return to her good graces. A stream of diplomats, many of whom had forgotten her address in the past two years, came to call. As I was departing, Mrs Gandhi asked me whether I would join her Cabinet. I told her that my regard for her was not based on anticipation of any rewards. I did not need a job and I was quite happy living in England. She then suggested that I become High Commissioner in Britain. Later on, I was offered other government positions, none of which I accepted. I did, however, assure Mrs Gandhi that I was always available to assist her in any way possible and she could count on my loyalty and support always.

Mrs Gandhi took me at my word. In the next four years she was in frequent contact with me by telephone. On several of her foreign trips, notably to Zimbabwe, Norway, Yugoslavia and the United States, I joined her official party. I was also now a regular visitor to India. In whatever way possible, I tried to be of help. On numerous matters, some small and some of considerable significance, Mrs Gandhi was in touch, and I found myself giving much time to these activities. One of them was the Festival of India in Britain. This was the first of several country-specific exhibitions to make the arts and crafts of India known around the world. As a Trustee of the Festival and Chairman of the Finance Committee, I saw this remarkable event take shape. Mrs Gandhi's official visit for the inauguration in March 1982 was in marked contrast to her trip in 1978—full of protocol and formalities, and the subservience that power brings. As always, she was the soul of consideration. The day before her departure was kept free of engagements. To my surprise, she said she was coming to my home for lunch and to spend some time with our family. Mrs Gandhi even recommended me for the Padma Bhushan, one of India's highest honours, which was bestowed by the President of India in January 1983. It was announced without the usual notification—I later learned that she had told her staff it was not necessary to obtain the formalities of acceptance because she wanted it to be unexpected. As of now, I am told I am the only Indian recipient of this award from outside India.

The last phase of Mrs Gandhi's life was dominated by three sequences of events, none of them pleasant. The first of these was full of tragedy. On Mrs Gandhi's return to office in 1980, it was obvious that Sanjay was scheduled to play a major role as her key political aide. He was now General Secretary of the Congress Party, Member of Parliament, and lived under the same roof as his mother. He had also begun to put his key henchmen, most of them younger neophytes, in critical positions, and had organized a sizeable group of parliamentarians into a Sanjay caucus. Then, in June, it was all over. Sanjay died as he lived— pushing things to the limit and taking risks. His small plane spun out of control and crashed while he was performing aerobatics. I flew immediately to Delhi and saw how devastated Mrs Gandhi was. She had not only lost a son, but also a political ally, a party manager, a tough street fighter and a possible successor. Her public composure was incredible. Somehow she went through the funeral and memorial ceremonies without collapsing.

I had another experience of her extraordinary graciousness. The funeral took place in blazing Delhi summer heat. I was tired and jet-lagged but was seated close to the family mourners. Suddenly, I fainted. In the midst of all the demands made on her, Mrs Gandhi was incredibly concerned and kind. She did everything possible to see that I was well looked after and comfortable. The next day, at another mourning, she kept whispering to a close associate: 'Keep an eye on Swraj.'

The fourth day after Sanjay's death, she was back in the Prime Minister's Office. I was one of the first callers. We shared some sad moments. I reminded her of my own sorrow with my daughter and how concentration on work helped me to survive. She quoted her father, who once said: 'Public figures cannot afford personal tragedies.' She added: 'I have never known, until today, the real meaning of this phrase.' Then, both Mrs Gandhi and I shed tears.

Sanjay was a difficult person to know. He had been intemperate and needlessly forceful during the Emergency. However, three hard years under constant Janata attack had seasoned him. By 1980, he was as strong-willed as ever, but more balanced and less given to rash judgements and actions. Because his personal style and manner was so different from that of his mother and grandfather, most Indians were unable to quite understand him. This was a young man in a hurry, generally given to short cuts, but he was also somebody who was scrupulous about keeping his word and told you exactly what he felt. He did not have the inclination for those time-wasting pleasantries that are such a distinctive feature of Indian society, a tendency which was variously mistaken for arrogance or rudeness. A vegetarian who did not smoke or drink, Sanjay's way of life was unaffected and basic. If he had lived and grown in maturity, the modern history of India would probably have been different.

Sanjay's death brought Mrs Gandhi closer to his infant son, Varun. She now doted on this baby and treated him with special love and care. Her daughter-in-law Maneka and the child continued to reside in her house, in rooms next to her own. Unfortunately, differences developed between the older and the younger Mrs Gandhi. Mrs Gandhi believed Maneka was using her son as a pressure point and this was heart-breaking for a grieving grandmother. Tensions escalated between Maneka, on the one hand, and Rajiv and Sonia on the other.

Since they all lived together and ate communal meals, it was an increasingly unhappy atmosphere. There were regular and unseemly disagreements. Soon, it became apparent that Maneka would leave the household and take Varun with her. Things came to a head in 1982. When Mrs Gandhi was in London opening the Festival of India, Maneka decided to go. The news reached Mrs Gandhi just as I called to accompany her to the Indo-British Association dinner at which she and Mrs Thatcher were guests of honour. I could see the distress and shock. The Prime Minister was suddenly a wounded grandmother who knew that her beloved grandchild would be withheld from her. Yet, she kept calm throughout the evening and made a very effective and unrehearsed speech. Mrs Gandhi was never quite the same again after Sanjay's death and her continuing unhappiness was worsened by Maneka's behaviour.

Sanjay's death began the political rise of Rajiv. Mrs Gandhi's elder son had been eclipsed by his younger brother and had been kept out of the political vortex. But no sooner had Sanjay passed away than there were moves to bring Rajiv in. The conventional perception is that Rajiv was reluctant and that it took a long time to persuade him to come forward. Much was made in the media, at home and abroad, about his unwillingness to enter political life. For over twelve months this coy cat-and-mouse game continued until Rajiv finally consented and won Sanjay's parliamentary seat at a by-election in June 1981. In fact, all this was a charade. I believe that Rajiv was as keen to enter politics as Mrs Gandhi was to get him in. This was quite visible to me well before Rajiv and Sonia came to London for the wedding of Prince Charles and Princess Diana in July 1981. This trip was so arranged as to give Rajiv some carefully selected exposure to British journalists and other notables. He met with several members of the House of Commons, called on Mrs Thatcher at Downing Street and addressed the Indo-British Association. Quite consciously, he cultivated a style which contrasted with that of his brother, a more suave, cosmopolitan approach with subtle inferences that the Emergency would not have happened if he had had any say in it. It was the image of the good son against the bad son! The way was being prepared.

From late 1981 until Mrs Gandhi's death on 31

October 1984, Rajiv's influence steadily expanded. And another parallel government came into being. This multiplied the infighting around Mrs Gandhi in both her official and private households. The parallel government became more and more important. Senior ministers and bureaucrats began courting Rajiv. A faction in the Prime Minister's Office, led by one of her senior aides, was seen to take orders from Rajiv rather than Mrs Gandhi. Another loyalist faction of people close to her resisted this. The hostility was open and Mrs Gandhi herself was well aware of it. Rajiv's own staff and associates were increasingly interfering. Mrs Gandhi's circle of close friends was also divided and a lot of her time was exhausted in mediating between one tale-carrier and another.

The growth of this parallel government gave unmerited prominence to a cluster of friends and associates around Rajiv. They enjoyed privileges without responsibility and appeared more powerful than members of the official administration. These young men seemed to be interested in only three things, including demonstrating how close they were to Rajiv and building his public aura, sometimes even at the expense of Mrs Gandhi's stature. It was obvious that they were encouraged by their patron.

Mrs Gandhi did nothing overt to correct matters, although I know that this was a source of considerable discomfort to her. There seems to be a weakness in many Indian leaders which causes problems of this nature. They should never exist in a democracy.

A third nasty development during Mrs Gandhi's final tenure was the Punjab situation. Events there had been deteriorating and lawlessness abounded. Various militant groups were sheltering in the Golden Temple in Amritsar. Something had to be done. A decision was made to assault the Temple and the army moved in. This led directly to the assassination which ended Mrs Gandhi's life a few months later. A stream of books and articles have examined all this and there is no need to elaborate further. But there is one part of the picture of which few are aware. It is how deeply Mrs Gandhi agonized over the decision to attack the sacred centre of the Sikhs. I am convinced that she was pushed into authorizing it by a few advisers who believed in a quick military strike to end Sikh resistance. Time and again, both before and after the action, she privately expressed her doubts, at one point saying: 'This will be war, and it's the worst kind of war—against our own people.' Things had become intolerable, but if Mrs Gandhi had followed her own instincts the outcome might have been quite different.

On several occasions in 1984 I urged the Prime Minister to be careful about her security. She had always resisted protection saying that it kept her away from her followers. As she put it: 'In a democracy, leaders cannot hide from their voters.' Indeed, she relished mass contact and had no inhibitions about plunging into the crowds which often surrounded her on political occasions. Her energies were recharged through such exchanges. It is ironic that death came at the hands of security guards—she was probably safer with the masses! Mrs Gandhi, who felt that she was somewhat psychic, had a lurking premonition of a violent end. In a way she accepted it as part of the price that leaders have to pay in turbulent times, and she took a rather fatalistic attitude whenever she was warned about threats to her person.

On 31 October 1984, at 4.30 a.m., I was awakened by a call from a friend in New York who had heard a newsflash that Mrs Gandhi had been shot and wounded. My contacts in Delhi confirmed these terrible tidings. I rushed to the airport and caught the first available plane to New Delhi. On the flight we were told that Mrs Gandhi had expired and that Rajiv had been appointed Prime Minister. My thoughts were quite disorientated and the journey seemed endless. I was too shocked to say or do much. Through my mind flashed remembrances of things past. India had lost its leader, but I had lost a guide and a friend.

Arriving in Delhi, I went directly to the Prime Minister's house. There I sat with her family in the room to which Mrs Gandhi's body had been brought from the hospital. Her face, amidst the flowers, seemed still to be racked with pain. Numb and speechless, I wondered why this tragedy had happened. Grief, I had learned years ago, has no explanation. One accepts it, but cannot explain it. I know that I went through all the motions at the funeral and afterwards. Yet, looking back, it is all a blur, a grey memory from another world. In 1984, I had written a book about Mrs Gandhi, an early copy of which she autographed for me. I concluded it with these words: 'Indira Gandhi became, if I may be forgiven for saying so, the personal incarnation of my love for the country of my birth; the personification of my hopes for its future; the strong symbol of the Indian people's continuing relationship with the country of my adoption.' This remains true.

Indira Gandhi was far from perfect. She would have been the first to admit that. Yet, with whatever shortcomings she may have had, she was an outstanding leader during a very complex and difficult era. She was a passionate nationalist: India and its preservation was the bedrock of her political thinking. Few Indians have such faith in their country, such pride in its heritage and achievements, and such identification with its ethos. In whatever she undertook, these sentiments were ever present. During her stewardship, she laboured mightily to protect the territorial integrity and independence of the nation.

She was also a responsible Prime Minister, worried about fiscal stability, security and order. When she died, the external debt was $9 billion—an amount she considered excessive. Today, it is around $120 billion!

Leadership does not take place in a vacuum. Leaders are human beings, and Mrs Gandhi was very human. Lodged in that humanity were two deep and persisting conflicts, which not only affected her inner self but also spilled over into her public life. One was a struggle between temperament and intellect. By personality, Mrs Gandhi was quite authoritarian, conscious of descent from a long line of Kashmiri brahmins, feeling a sense of family pride which inspired both a commitment to leadership and a feeling that leadership was theirs by right of service. She was immensely disciplined and believed that all others should be. Yet, through her readings, interests and lifelong associations, she was a liberal in her mental outlook and values. There was a constant clash between these two elements of her being. Never quite comfortable with either, she leaned sometimes one way, sometimes another. Yet, she generally accepted democracy, if not out of total conviction, at least out of the belief that it was good for India.

A second tension, particularly in Mrs Gandhi's later years, sprang from the inconsistencies inherent in her dual roles, that of a national leader and that of a mother. As her sons became involved in politics, this was a balance she found difficult to reconcile, something made worse by the ambitions of her children. Here again, she was intellectually convinced that there was no contradiction in these roles, that Sanjay and Rajiv would earn their political preferment on merit and after adequate apprenticeship. Yet, in her heart, she knew well that things did not work this way and it was a gnawing concern.

The lasting impression which Mrs Gandhi leaves is of a leader and a woman of indomitable courage. Her physical bravery was legendary. There was no danger of which she was afraid and no circumstances in which she could be intimidated. But there was something more than this. Mrs Gandhi had immense moral strength. When certain of her cause, there was no obstacle too daunting for her to confront. She was, in reality, a sensitive and vulnerable person who overcame the hurts and barbs of decades of rough politics, one who had to build a protective wall around her feelings. Her sense of duty was exemplary and she paid a heavy price for it. Mrs Gandhi was convinced of her destiny and, in this spirit, she met her fate.

8

Investing in India

The Indian economy is a sleeping giant. For several decades, there have been frequent discussions on how to awaken it—how to enliven an economy which should be one of the largest and most powerful in the world but has been a consistent underperformer. Most economists, planners and others concerned with these things have argued that the only way to induce dynamic growth is to unshackle the economy from the chains of protection, the regulatory restrictions which keep it closed, inefficient and inward-looking. During the past fifteen years or so, a succession of governments have spoken of liberalization, reform, opening doors and increasing competitiveness. The results have been meagre because the efforts have been tentative. Sometimes, these thrusts have been only theoretical and sometimes more positive, as has happened since 1991. But, overall, they are limited and half-hearted.

The delays, obstructions and subversions which have attended reform programmes have profoundly damaged the economic prospects of India. If such policies had been implemented years ago, they would surely have put India into the big league of the world economy, bringing considerable prosperity and assuring a rise of living standards similar to that of East Asia. Why, then, a reluctance to implement measures widely accepted as beneficial to the country?

The answer lies in the nexus that exists between economic power and political power in India. A closed economy breeds its own defences. It spawns small but influential corporate groups who protect their illegal privileges by suborning political leaders. The favourable treatment which they get includes heavy government investment in their enterprises and protection of their inefficient, and often corrupt, businesses from the competition and transparency that a more open economy brings. In short, this bunch of tycoons are quite prepared to damage the national interest to promote personal interests—morally criminal ends which are generally pursued through physically criminal means! The methods they deploy include a range of inducements to politicians, senior bureaucrats and supportive journalists, and intimidation of those who resist them.

The Indian economy does not generate sufficient wealth to underwrite its own programme of modernization. The old semi-socialist and protective regimen has also been unable to attract much capital to India. Without such flows to regenerate the economy, India will either limp along or will need to borrow huge amounts of expensive capital which will not be properly utilized in a sheltered environment. Obviously, then, a central purpose of policy must be to find ways of attracting the least costly capital from abroad, and of harnessing the new technologies and methodologies that it will bring. It is only far-reaching reforms that can create the conditions which will enable this.

In these circumstances, it is natural that primary consideration be given to the resources of non-resident Indians (NRIs). There are currently about twenty million individuals of Indian origin living outside India. Each year, their collective economic output is at least equal to the gross domestic product of India. Their accumulated savings total from around $700 billion to $1 trillion. Although it is a constant topic of discussion and anticipation by economists and planners, this huge pool of capital has hardly been tapped. It represents a formidable source of funds with a generic interest in India. What is more, it can be a lightning rod for other non-Indian money which is much more likely to follow if NRI investments lead the way.

This is the concept which led me to make six major investment attempts in India 1983 onwards. Each of them was in response to government initiatives, undertaken in the belief that the proclaimed reform efforts were genuine and would embrace both the technicalities of investment as well as the ethos of business. The enormous sensation surrounding some of my moves, and the obstacles affecting others, now make me feel that a real commitment to sustained and comprehensive reform has still to come. My own efforts are symbolic of a larger concern: I feel that without enlightened policies and their purposeful pursuit, the economic future of India is in doubt. The waywardness, indecision, insincerity and sporadic nature of reforms has imposed an incalculable burden on the well-being of the Indian people.

Unable to run a state-dominated system effectively, and unwilling to fully ventilate it with with an open and competitive approach, the country has been condemned to economic mediocrity. Let me discuss this further through the medium of my own experiences.

*

The first of my investments—probably the most controversial happening in recent Indian business history—was in two leading industrial companies situated in Delhi: DCM and Escorts. It began in this way. Following her return to office in January 1980, Mrs Gandhi had been interested in encouraging greater NRI involvement in the Indian economy. There were two reasons for this: her emotional instinct that NRIs should be linked to their motherland, and her desire to improve the economy. She was extremely dissatisfied with the minuscule return on capital by the state-owned businesses, and she realized that Indian private enterprise—which she described as 'more private than enterprising'—was not globally competitive or domestically dynamic. Her advisers accordingly formulated several proposals, one of which was designed to open existing companies to portfolio investment by NRIs. Until then, there was an almost complete ban on anyone from outside India buying existing shares in Indian companies. Now, non-resident Indians could buy such shares, so could companies controlled by them, provided the monies used in these transactions were remitted through state-owned Indian banks.

Initially, Indian managements were enthusiastic about the prospect of NRI stock investment. In October 1982, a high-powered delegation of business leaders visited London to promote their shares to NRIs. The group included H.P. Nanda, Chairman of Escorts, and Bharat Ram, Chairman of DCM. It was led by L.K. Jha, a former senior civil servant and diplomat who was Chairman of the Indian Economic Administrative Reforms Commission. There was a meeting with NRIs at India House and a vigorous attempt to promote purchases of shares in Indian companies. One of the arguments used was that the shares of bigger businesses were listed on the stock exchanges in India and so provided investor liquidity. I did not attend this event because I had no interest in investing in India at that time. In general, the response to this delegation in Britain and the other countries they visited was poor. NRIs were rather indifferent.

The most senior economic officials of the government enthusiastically supported the new policy. In November 1982, a Convention of the Overseas

The original Apeejay House, the Paul family home in Jalandhar where it all began.

Swraj Paul at MIT, Boston, 1952.

At the Institute's metallurgy laboratory.

Swraj and Aruna Paul on their wedding day, 1 December 1956.

With HRH Prince Charles at the opening of Natural Gas Tubes Factory at Tredegar, South Wales, 3 June 1977.

With Mrs Indira Gandhi at Tredegar, 16 November 1978.

Swraj Paul speaking at the Indo-British Association dinner in honour of Prime Ministers Indira Gandhi and Margaret Thatcher on 23 March 1982.

Swraj Paul being presented with the Padma Bhushan
by the President of India, Giani Zail Singh, 2 April
1983.

With former Labour Party Leader John Smith at a concert to commemorate
Surrendra Paul at the House of Commons on 27 October 1990.

Swraj Paul after being awarded on honorary degree in Economics at the University of Hull, 10 July 1992. With him are Aruna Paul, sons Angad, Akash and Ambar, daughters in-law Gauri and Nisha, and Deputy High Commissioner and Mrs K.V. Rajan.

Swraj Paul with sons Akash, Angad and Ambar and Prime Minister John Major at the Caparo Group twenty-fifth anniversary celebrations in Huntingdon, 11 February 1994.

With former Labour Party Leaders Neil Kinnock and Michael Foot at the Toynbee Prize Giving and Lecture, 25 November 1994.

Swraj Paul with Prime Minister Tony Blair of Britain.

Lord Paul in the full regalia of a peer after his elevation to the House of Lords in October 1996.

Swraj and Aruna Paul with their four children, two daughters-in-law and six grandchildren at London Zoo, 1996.

At the opening of the Baroness Paul Pygmy Hippo Enclosure, London Zoo, 29 June 1997. The Lord Paul; The Rt Hon Lord Richard, Leader of the House of Lords, The Rt Hon Frank Dobson, MP, Secretary of State for Health; Baroness Paul; and Mr Richard Burge, Director-General, Zoological Society of London.

Swraj Paul kisses son Angad at the ground-breaking ceremony for the Caparo Maruti plant at Gurgaon near Delhi on 25 July 1994. Looking on are (left) R.C. Bhargava, who was then Managing Director of Maruti Udyog and, at right, M.D. Jindal.

Admiring cartoonist Sudhir Telang's rendering of him at a function in New Delhi; 5 January 1997.

With Prime Minister Inder Kumar Gujral at the convention of non-resident Indians held in New Delhi on 22 December 1997.

Ambika Paul

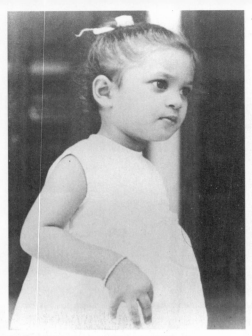

The Ambika Paul memorial at Caparo Steel, Farrell, Pennsylvania, installed in November 1995.

AMBIKA PAUL

12th NOVEMBER 1963 TO 19th APRIL 1968

Ambika Paul was born in Calcutta, the second daughter and fourth child of Swraj and Aruna Paul. For the first two years of her life she lived happily with her family in India. But that happiness was short lived when, aged only two, she was found to have leukaemia. Ambika's parents brought her to London for the most advanced medical treatment available, although they had been told there was no cure. She was admitted to the Middlesex Hospital where, for the next two years, every effort was made to save her. But her family never gave up hope for, in spite of her terrible illness, Ambika's bravery and love of life were an inspiration to everyone who knew her.

Whenever she had a break from the medical treatment, her parents would bring her to London Zoo to see the animals that she loved so much. The Zoo was a very special place to Ambika and the hours that she spent with her family in these gardens were among the most joyful of her short life. Sadly, Ambika died on 19th April 1968.

Her family never returned to India, choosing instead to live in London where they felt closer to Ambika and, over the next twenty five years, they built up a successful industrial empire, the Caparo Group.

In 1992, when London Zoo announced that it was in danger of closing, the Paul family offered a one million pound donation to build a new Children's Zoo and the Ambika Paul Memorial Gardens. They believe the Zoo to be the kind of place where parents and children can truly enjoy each other's company, and it is their hope that the love and affection Ambika inspired will be a source of happiness for many other families in the years to come. The Ambika Paul Memorial Gardens and Children's Zoo are an expression of love and grateful thanks from her family.

Swraj Paul has said: "Ambika was an angel who changed our lives. The vision which has guided us was born in those terrible days. My wife, Aruna, who has always been such a tower of strength to me, shares this thought of our destiny being forged through tragedy".

This plaque was unveiled by
Swraj Paul, Chairman, Caparo Group of companies, and Aruna Paul,
Amber, Akash, Anjli, Angad
12th November 1994.

The plaque at London Zoo in memory of Ambika. The zoo was in danger of closing down in 1992 when the Paul family helped financially.

The Ambika Paul fountain at Regent's Park Zoo, London.

Indian Jaambo Association in Bombay was addressed by Manmohan Singh, then Governor of the Reserve Bank of India and much later Finance Minister. Singh's endorsement of NRI portfolio investments was complete: '. . . another class of investors may not like to expose their funds to risks and uncertainties of investing in new ventures, but may like to purchase, through a stock exchange, shares of companies with proven worth.

'A portfolio investment scheme has been devised to cater for the needs of such investors who can purchase, through a recognized stock exchange, shares of any company.' He went on to outline the scheme and the streamlined procedures which would enable investors to remit funds and also secure repatriation of them. Nothing could be more explicit, coming as it did from the chief central banker in the land.

On 18 December 1982, I was flying to India for the holidays and met L.K. Jha on the plane. Jha discussed NRI portfolio investment and urged me to buy some shares: 'Swraj, if people like you who are so involved with India are not going to invest, who will?' I reflected on his invitation and thought I would make a modest investment. My brother Jit introduced me to Harish Bhasin, a well-known broker who was also Chairman of the Stockbrokers Association in Delhi. I asked Bhasin whether there were any good Indian companies which merited investment. He told me that, in Delhi, there were really only two worthwhile enterprises—DCM and Escorts. I asked him to buy a few shares and send me their balance sheets. Back in London, my examination of their financial statements was hardly enlightening. They had the minimum of information with the maximum of public relations. The auditors reports were lengthy and complicated, unlike the reports that investors find in public company balance sheets in the Western world.

Between January and March 1983 I was, of course, in London. I continued to study these two companies carefully and obtained more information on them. I asked Bhasin to find out the extent of the shareholdings of the reputed owning families. His response was that the Shri Rams, who held all the senior management positions at DCM, had only a small holding of their own. He also told me that the Nandas, who similarly dominated Escorts, held the majority of their company's shares. It seemed to me that, if I acquired significant holdings, I could push DCM's management into improving the performance of their company, for which there was much scope. If they did not respond, they could be replaced with competent professionals. Either way, the share value would increase considerably. I told Bhasin to buy as many shares of DCM as were available. Because of his information about the major size of the Nanda family's ownership, I did not immediately pursue Escorts further.

In April 1983, I visited Delhi again. While there, I met Rajiv Gandhi, who had recently become a Member of Parliament. Among other things, I told him what I was doing on the stock market. His response was remarkable. Rajiv got quite excited and urged me to buy as much as possible. 'Buy DCM, buy Escorts, buy

Mahindra and Tisco' (two other major corporations). 'They are not with us and we should control them.'

I told him that DCM was a possibility, but that the Nandas owned too much of Escorts for any outsider to make an impact. Also, I indicated that I was in no hurry to rush into buying shares in many other companies. The next day, to my surprise, he called me on the phone to say that he had checked the Nanda holdings and, in fact, they held only a minor ownership position. I investigated this further and found that Rajiv was correct. So, I now instructed Bhasin to buy whatever he could in both DCM and Escorts. As these purchases took place, the stock price of both companies escalated—and several board directors and members of the Shri Ram and Nanda families were selling shares, entranced by their rising value.

At this point, Rajiv Gandhi introduced me to Vivek Bharat Ram, Deputy Managing Director of DCM and son of its Chairman, and said: 'Swraj owns these shares in your company. He will be able to help you and you can do business with him.' I never heard from Vivek again, but he was clearly in touch with Rajiv, who had been a schoolmate. By mid-April, the news had got around that it was Swraj Paul who was buying the DCM and Escorts shares. The result was amazing: sheer panic among the Shri Rams and Nandas. The corporate establishment in India also seemed thunderstruck and rushed to give solace to both families. J.R.D. Tata, the high panjandrum of Indian business, gasped: 'I could be next!' The then President of the Federation of Indian Chambers of

Commerce & Industry (FICCI), was rallying members to the defence of the alarmed Shri Ram and Nanda clans.

By this time, I had acquired 13 per cent of all DCM shares. The Shri Ram family jointly controlled 10 per cent. Another 42.5 per cent was held by public financial institutions—insurance companies, development banks and unit trusts owned by the government. My Escorts holdings were 7.5 per cent of the total, while the Nandas controlled less than 5 per cent—and financial institutions owned 54.9 per cent. I had now many more shares than either of the two families who had controlled the managements for decades. The fear which haunted the Nandas and Shri Rams was that, together with the financial institutions, I could drive them from their plush jobs and call them to account for the way in which they ran their companies. Working in concert with their friends and supporters, the Nandas and Shri Rams now devised a campaign to stop me. I was soundly denounced in the media, sections of the business community rose up against me, my shares were not registered and attempts were made to turn senior bureaucrats and ministers and even Rajiv Gandhi against me.

By the middle of April, I was back in London. But the campaign was getting into high gear in India. Newspapers and journals suddenly began carrying articles abusing me and making a number of insulting insinuations.

I was called a crook, a nomad, a master of shady deals, a brown Englishman, an upstart, a speculator, a recycler of black cash and illegal funds, a purveyor of tainted funds, and so on. Well-known financial writers, later called 'purchasable commodities' by me, began publishing obviously inspired articles. Allegations were made that I was using Mrs Gandhi's money to buy DCM and Escorts. Attempts were made to dig for dirt about me and my family. Sadly for the investigators, nothing was found. These murky tactics must have cost the perpetrators millions of rupees.

Meetings were held to denounce NRIs in general and my stock purchases in particular. A group from FICCI requested an interview with Mrs Gandhi to discuss Swraj Paul, a request she very properly turned down. Another delegation, including H.P. Nanda, Bharat Ram and other business barons, and led by Tata himself, called on Finance Minister Pranab Mukherjee on 20 April 1983. Their purpose was to seek protection. The very businessmen who were soliciting NRI purchases of their shares in the autumn of 1982 were now screaming against what they had so anxiously wanted.

H.P. Nanda, Bharat Ram, their sons and agents targetted key government officials. Then, on 26 April, the very man who urged NRI portfolio investment with all the authority of his office just six months earlier, spoke. Addressing the National Productivity Council in New Delhi, Reserve Bank Governor Manmohan Singh said: '. . . it is necessary to protect well-managed companies against takeover bids from abroad.' Singh added that Indian industry was entitled to 'an assurance from the government that we shall not allow enterprises in India to become a bubble on the whirlpool of international speculation'. Orchestrated press support greeted this pronouncement. I was surprised to learn about this change in policy. Dr Manmohan Singh was known to be a person anxious to encourage NRI investment, as he did during his tenure as Finance Minister in 1991–96. What was it that caused his sudden shift at that time?

Manmohan Singh's about-face presaged a major change in Reserve Bank policy. The Reserve Bank now declared that all past purchases of shares by NRI investors should have had their specific permission and that it was not sufficient to merely have sent funds through an Indian bank for this purpose.

The Punjab National Bank, a state-owned institution, then pointed out that these requirements were retroactive and consequently could not apply to my transactions, that this was policy enforced backwards in time. In June and July, the Reserve Bank also proceeded to request a large amount of needless information about my own businesses in London. Until this was answered, they would hold up payment of monies to my broker, Bhasin, from the Punjab National Bank, through whom it was remitted. This unusual move, in contradiction of earlier Reserve Bank rules, was obviously designed to prevent any further purchase of shares. After a long exchange of telexes, in which I pointed out the discriminatory and abnormal nature of their requests, the Bank desisted. Although ultimately fruitless, the signal sent out by the Bank's reversal of policy was evident—Swraj Paul was to be blocked.

I complained about this reversal of Reserve Bank policy to Mrs Gandhi and asked whether it reflected a shift in government policy. Mrs Gandhi was puzzled and asked for an explanation. It became clear that there were all sorts of machinations going on without Mrs Gandhi's knowledge. Now that she had been alerted, it was clear from her later comments to me, and a few others, that she would have followed through and investigated the matter thoroughly; but then she was tragically killed.

One of the most serious, and ultimately, self-defeating, moves by DCM and Escorts was their refusal to register the shares I had purchased. Shares openly transacted on the stock market are usually registered promptly, with the purchaser listed as the new owner. On 9 June 1983 the board of Escorts met and decided to refuse transfer of the shares I had bought. On 15 July, the DCM board also refused. This behaviour upset many people. Stockholders were incensed, small shareholders were deeply troubled, segments of the financial press began to raise objections, and government authorities were becoming worried. Even the venerable J.R.D. Tata saw this as a mistake and had to assure the annual general meeting of the Tata Iron & Steel Company (TISCO) that his companies fully recognized the free transferability of their shares listed on the stock exchanges.

In order to further demonstrate that they did not recognize my ownership, DCM and Escorts made things worse for themselves by continuing to pay dividends to the former owners of these shares—former owners who had long sold their holdings. The financial institutions were aghast and, after some internal discussions, demanded that shares duly purchased be registered. This DCM and Escorts still refused to do.

In all this, the role of Rajiv Gandhi was inexplicable. In April and the early summer of 1983, he was very supportive, even pressing me to acquire more shares. But somewhere around late summer 1983 it seems as though DCM and Escorts had been able to reach out to him. And to this date, I am not quite sure what changed. However, there are several possible reasons to which I attribute this reversal of attitude: his discomfort at the inordinate fuss which was being raised by DCM and Escorts; his growing realization that I would not bend to his every whim had I taken control of the companies; and possibly other considerations. Later, in November that year, Rajiv made a statement on the floor of the Lok Sabha saying that no NRI should be allowed to own more than 2 per cent of the shares of any Indian company. Yet, he was simultaneously telling me that this was not meant for me and he was not against what I was doing!

Mrs Gandhi, on the other hand, was quite categorical, in public and private, that government policy remained what it had been and that NRI investments were welcome. She said this so forcefully at a meeting with NRIs in New York on her visit in autumn 1983 that it was construed as a clear statement of support for me. When asked if this was so, her reply was, 'You can interpret it as you like, but I stand by government policy which is unchanged.'

The final element in the stop-Swraj strategy of the Shri Rams and Nandas was sponsorship of a committee of supposedly non-resident Indian investors in London. Their activities were largely confined to issuing press releases saying that NRIs must create new industrial ventures and not make portfolio investments in India. This was so patently a back-door propaganda channel that it lacked any credibility and duly expired. Yet, it demonstrated the lengths to which DCM and Escorts would go. In their hostility, they failed to see that some London NRIs were using them to try and obtain acceptance by the business establishment in India!

While all this was under way, I was investigating the workings of both DCM and Escorts. The more I learned of what was going on, the more unhappy I was with the way these companies were run.

I began expressing my views in a series of questions and statements which I made public. They were widely read in the Indian press. An amusing sideline of these revelations was the family discords which they provoked. Many of the senior executives in big companies had given their wives and children the impression that they owned the businesses themselves. When the paucity of their holdings was disclosed, spouses were furious—husbands had vastly overstated their wealth, and these deceptions were not taken lightly by their wives! After years of boasting about their ownership of companies, it was not easy for these men to explain to their families that they they were actually worth very much less than they had proclaimed.

In the face of all this, I had to defend myself. I determined to do this as directly as possible. For six weeks in July and August 1983, I visited India. I gave dozens of speeches, interviews, and statements. It was like an election campaign conducted in the financial centres of the country—Bombay, Calcutta and Delhi. The response was incredible. Literally thousands of interested individuals contacted me or came to hear me speak. Most of them were small shareholders in large public companies who had been virtually disenfranchised by managements. Others were concerned citizens who felt that corporate wrongdoers were looting the country. A large number of junior journalists, disgusted at the way in which their seniors and their employers were toadying to big business, gave me their unstinted support. Young people everywhere urged me to continue. Owners of small- and medium-sized businesses were very enthusiastic. They told me that, at long last, somebody had challenged the monopoly interests which dominated Indian business and opposed competition. Many employees of big companies, including DCM and Escorts, give me their quiet endorsements. Even a few of the more liberal-minded big businessmen called to extend their good wishes, albeit cautiously and not too openly! It was an outpouring of encouragement which sustained me against the cascade of vilification undertaken by the business establishment. In these unpleasant times, my late brother, Surrendra, was of enormous and courageous assistance.

I spoke out very frankly. My argument was that my personal situation was simply symbolic of what large business interests were doing to the country: grossly misusing public money and capital provided by unsuspecting shareholders. Without regard to their management performance, many corporate maharajas were taking a ride on public funds. Their arrogance was seen in the unwillingness to register my shares and the high-handed refusal to answer basic questions. I pointed out that this was a national issue and asked: Can a handful of people downgrade a country? On 6 August 1983 well over two thousand people gathered to listen to my address to the All India Investors Association in Bombay. My speech (quoted in *Appendix I*) gave a comprehensive analysis of my position. After this meeting the *Sunday Observer* asked me why I was being treated like a popular filmstar. My reply was this: 'Because, for the first time, a businessman is calling a spade a spade . . . a handful have got together and are trying to beat one poor little man. And this is the first time they have not been able to cow down a person!'

When I left India in late August, public opinion was strongly in my favour. DCM and Escorts had begun to understand that mud-slinging was not working. But they still refused to register my shares and now devised new tactics.

On 18 September 1983 the Reserve Bank issued a circular confirming existing government policy on NRI investment, but stating that such investment made *after* 2 May 1983 could not exceed 5 per cent of the total equity capital of any Indian company. This, in effect, fully legitimized my purchases of shares which were all made before that date. Soon after this circular, Escorts—fearing that the government would now direct them to register legally acquired shares—went to court. By Writ Petition No. 3063 of 1983, they requested the Bombay High Court to declare the Reserve Bank circular 'illegal and void' as it contravened the Foreign Exchange Regulation Act—a law which placed restrictions on overseas monetary transactions. Several agencies of the government responded. The Ministry of Finance, the Reserve Bank (through its Controller of Exchange) and the Punjab National Bank, all denied Escorts' allegations. The case proceeded in the usual protracted way common in Indian judicial matters.

A little later, Chairman H.P. Nanda announced that Escorts was planning a new issue of Rs. 35 crores (350 million) in shares and debentures. This would result in a dilution of the holdings of the financial institutions, who owned more than one-half of the Escorts shares. The institutions, who saw this as a scheme to reduce the significance and value of their shares, were enraged. They were handling public funds and their officers would be derelict in their duty if they did not resist. This they did. Two routes were open for their protest.

Any new issue of this magnitude needed the approval of existing shareholders as well as, at the time, the Controller of Capital Issues—a government official who supervised the capital structure of public companies. The institutions would inform him that they opposed Nanda's plan. They also served notice that they would seek to replace a majority of the Escorts board of directors, a procedure they were entitled to follow since they were major shareholders. Escorts went to court to stop this.

My tussle with DCM–Escorts and my acquisition of shares became a parliamentary issue. Two members of the Opposition, J.B. Mathur and R.R. Murarka, alleged in Parliament that I was investing Mrs Gandhi's money hidden in Swiss banks. Mrs Gandhi made a stern denial in the Lok Sabha, but I did not have access to the same forum. I denounced Mathur and Murarka in the press, pointing out that if their remarks had been made in public, they would be subject to libel and defamation laws. Parliamentary privilege was being used to propagate flagrant lies. Mathur and Murarka, not daring to make this statement outside the legislature, charged me with violating the rights of members and insulting Parliament. I wrote a lengthy reply to the Speaker of Lok Sabha, arguing that the privileges of Parliamentarians depended on their responsible behaviour. Innocent individuals had no protection from members who abused the shelter of Parliament. A breach of privilege inquiry went on for a long time and eventually ended in nothing, but all this was quite a sensation in those days.

At the end of 1983 I was again in India. And once again, I took the opportunity to present my case to as wide an audience as possible. The response was even more supportive. At Delhi University, for instance, a large crowd of students gave me a rousing reception, empathizing with my position. Big things were also happening in Calcutta—the Congress Party was holding a major national committee meeting; an assembly of FICCI was taking place and the Calcutta

Stock Exchange was celebrating a jubilee, all at about the same time. As usual, I was spending my Christmas holidays with my family in the city. But this time, it was hardly a holiday! At the Congress Party sessions, Mrs Gandhi made it clear that she was deeply disappointed at the conduct of the business community and its contribution to national development. Finance Minister Mukherjee told the Calcutta Stock Exchange that the government would not remain a 'silent spectator' to a situation where investors were kept uncertain about the fate of shares purchased on the stock market. The Committee of the Presidents of Stock Exchanges declared that the power of companies to refuse registration should not be used in a 'capricious manner'. They warned of the impact on the investment climate of the country of withholding registration. Everywhere I went and spoke, the reception was highly favourable.

These matters dragged on through most of 1984. The law courts were taking their time. Although Mrs Gandhi and Mukherjee were positive, the government did little. I understand that the principal reason for this was Rajiv Gandhi, who was only an ordinary MP in name, but was acquiring increasing power over the workings of the administration. On the one hand, he was telling me that everything was all right and would soon work out well; on the other, he was doing as much as he could to assist those resisting me. In my presence, he would tell one of his senior aides that there was no reason for any delay in this matter and that it should be expedited. Yet the aide probably felt that to act would incur Rajiv's displeasure—no small threat at that time. Mrs Gandhi, however, remained supportive but I did not burden her with any extended discussions about this.

In mid-1984, I was again in India and, as usual, called on Mrs Gandhi. I found her distressed. She showed me a memorandum which Rajiv had sent to her about DCM–Escorts. In it, he accused me of being a conduit for money from one of her aides which had been used to buy DCM and Escorts shares. Mrs Gandhi said that she knew Rajiv's allegations were quite untrue. I could see how upset she was, so I told her to forget about it. This was the essence of the misery of her last years—she knew that what Rajiv said and did was often incorrect, yet she could not bring herself to confront him.

A member of parliament and, at that time, an intimate of Rajiv, says that Mrs Gandhi discussed the memorandum with him soon after my meeting with her. He, too, witnessed her mixture of anger and sorrow as she said to him: 'Tell Rajiv that once Nehrus make commitments they don't go back on their word.'

I was staying at the Taj Mahal Hotel when I received a telephone call from H.P. Nanda. He asked whether we could meet. When I asked him to come to the hotel, he suggested that we get together on more neutral ground. I told him that if his house was neutral enough, I would go there. At his residence I asked him to register my shares and run the company in a manner I deemed fit. Nanda was taken aback and replied that the way he managed the company was the way it was normally done in India. He said,

'Oh everybody does this.' My response was that I did not own shares in 'everybody' but I was a major investor in Escorts! The discussion ended and I never again heard from Nanda on this subject.

When Mrs Gandhi died in October, things were still unresolved. Then, the Bombay High Court delivered a verdict in favour of Escorts. Government officials and the financial institutions were anxious to appeal. There was pressure on them not to do so.

Rajiv Gandhi, who was the new Prime Minister, was apparently hesitant, but the determination of the institutions was unshakeable. Their position would have been subject to much criticism and their investments at risk if they did not challenge the High Court verdict. An appeal was lodged in the Supreme Court.

At the end of 1984, India went to the polls. I wrote to Rajiv, telling him that I was sure of a major Congress victory and that this would be the nation's final tribute to his mother. The election was a stunning triumph. In January 1985, I met with Rajiv in New Delhi. In the course of conversation, I reminded him of my letter and repeated that the electoral result was really Indira's last farewell. Rajiv did not like this. Encouraged by all around, he preferred to think that this was his own success. I then talked about the abrupt dismissal of R.K. Dhawan, which had taken place a few days earlier. Dhawan had been so loyal to Mrs Gandhi and would be useful to him, too. Rajiv was not impressed by this.

The DCM–Escorts situation meandered on through 1985. Litigation with Escorts continued. So did the public debate. Then, on 23 December, the Supreme Court delivered judgement. The High Court decision was reversed. The battle was over and Escorts had lost.

They were now directed to register my shares. The Nandas, and by extension the Shri Rams, would have to accept me as a full shareholder. This had just happened when another thunderbolt struck. H.P. Nanda and his son Rajan were re-appointed for five years as Chairman and Managing Director of Escorts respectively. These are corporate positions but they have to be confirmed by the Company Law Board, a government department. The appointments, the speed of their approval and its timing, indicated that the Nandas had been rescued by assistance from high places. The financial institutions and I were both shocked.

Rajiv was in Bombay and I was in Delhi. So I went to see Arun Nehru. He, too, was puzzled and called Rajiv. Nothing came of this meeting and so on 6 January 1986 I visited Rajiv at his residence. He pretended that he knew nothing about the re-appointment of the Nandas and said that we must find out who was responsible. His tone and manner showed his discomfort. He then said that I could sell my shares and he would see that no financial loss was suffered. There was no purpose in fighting the Prime Minister of India, so I agreed to this.

Rajiv immediately called Gopi Arora and another intimate of his, Arun Singh, Minister of State for Defence. A meeting was arranged in Arora's office with both of them. It was agreed that I would sell my shares to the Shri Rams and Nandas with no financial loss to me. When a senior bureaucrat and a minister get involved in negotiating share transactions on orders from their Prime Minister, it is indeed a strange world! The 'no loss' arrangement of 1986 proved to be fictional. Full repatriation of my capital took ten years—government permission for foreign exchange transfers was only given in dribs and drabs. There was no compensation for interest or for currency devaluation. Eventually, the cost to me was fifteen crore (150 million) rupees. And so, a dismal affair ended.

I had little confidence left in Rajiv. We still met occasionally, but he was increasingly oblivious to the truth and did not like being told it. In mid-1987, I called on him at the Waldorf Astoria Hotel in New York. I told him that the common impression was that he had received a commission on the Bofors arms deal. He should try to clear this up if his reputation was not to be irretrievably damaged. In December 1987 I repeated this to him in New Delhi. Such talk was unwelcome and I rarely saw Rajiv Gandhi thereafter. Bofors was his nemesis, and remains an unanswered question which haunts his posthumous reputation.

The DCM–Escorts experience had a beneficial long-term fallout. It contributed significantly to awakening shareholders to their rights, something in which there had been very little public involvement earlier. The power of companies to refuse registration has also come under scrutiny. It is unlikely that any major corporation can now adopt such tactics. The role and behaviour of financial institutions has been widely discussed. The financial press is more sensitive to malfeasance than it was before.

A great deal needs to be done in the area of management accountability and stock market reform, but I like to think that the DCM–Escorts controversy was a small beginning. A decade later, several journalists who were my critics acknowledge that what I did served that end.

The conclusion of this affair is tinged with sadness. H.P. Nanda and Bharat Ram soon retired. Escorts never quite recovered its reputation and the DCM group was carved up by a younger generation. Recently, the noted columnist Khushwant Singh wrote me a short letter which is a telling epitaph to this episode:

Sujan Singh Park
New Delhi
July 29, 1996

Dear Swraj Paul Ji,
A million thanks for your very kind letter. I am afraid my travelling days are fast coming to a close. I am 82. However, whenever you are in Delhi you will be more than welcome in our home. Bharat who was in school with us drops in once or twice a week. He now admits that what you were doing was quite legitimate.

Best of luck.

Yours sincerely
Khushwant Singh

While the DCM–Escorts activities were going on, I was also involved in a second investment. In the early

1980s, the Government of India decided that four large fertilizer plants were necessary. Accordingly, licences were given to four major industrial groups. One of them was DCM which, by 1984, had decided not to proceed.

In mid-1984, Mrs Gandhi told me about this and asked whether I could replace DCM. My answer was that if this was her wish, and it would help the country, then I was ready to go ahead. The project would have cost around $300 million in those days. I submitted a letter of application to the government, in accordance with the required procedures.

Mrs Gandhi died and nothing happened for a while. In mid-1985 I received a phone call in London from Vincent George, secretary to Rajiv Gandhi. He asked whether I was still interested in the project. I said I was. A few months later I was in Hawaii when George tracked me down and told me that the Prime Minister had cleared my application for the fertilizer plant and I could now proceed. My brothers and I incorporated an Indian company for this purpose and began the preparatory work. Soon, plant specifications were ready and competitive quotes were solicited for the equipment. Several manufacturers responded. One of them was Snam Progetti, an Italian firm. Snam Progetti's tender was about $35 million more than other offers. I also believed that their equipment was not the best in technological terms.

However, strenuous efforts were made to ensure that I purchased it. Ottavio Quattrocchi, their representative in India, told me that the Prime Minister wanted this technology used. The Minister of State in charge of fertilizers also strongly urged that we buy Snam's machinery and said the government was keen that we do so. I explained the cost and the technical problems to both Quattrocchi and the Minister, but they persisted. So, I went to see the Prime Minister and told him what was going on. He said I should buy the best and the cheapest, and ignore everything else. Different signals reached me from elsewhere. I was getting nowhere with the ministry. Personal meetings with Rajiv were fruitless. He merely repeated what he had said before, but obviously the same message was not getting to the fertilizer officials—whose approval was necessary before equipment could be bought.

In 1988, the licence for this project was up for renewal. Such extensions are usually automatically granted. The three other fertilizer manufacturers, who had all purchased Snam equipment, had their permits renewed. Without prior notification, mine was cancelled and promptly given elsewhere. My only regret is that I was unable to erect the kind of fertilizer facilities that India needs—and that with the cheapest and best technology.

*

My enthusiasm for doing business in India was somewhat dampened by these experiences. But, in 1991, things looked more promising. A much publicized reform programme had been announced by the government which said that that new technology was supposedly welcome. In July of that year the

Chief Minister of West Bengal was in London and asked me to help with economic development in his state. I have a high regard for Mr Jyoti Basu, who is a respected politician of principle. What he had in mind was the revival of the Indian Iron & Steel Company (IISCO), an old business located in Burnpur near Calcutta.

IISCO was a major operation which had been nationalized by the Government of India many years ago. It was managed by SAIL, the state-owned Steel Authority of India, was operating at 25 per cent of capacity, and was losing large amounts of money. Basu said that IISCO was almost bankrupt and was having difficulty in continuing. His own priority was the preservation of jobs. If some redundancy was necessary, it should be done with the cooperation of the workers and without animosity. The benefits of the revival of IISCO would have a considerable impact on the economy of West Bengal. I assured the Chief Minister that I was prepared to help.

Basu discussed this with the Central government. The Steel Ministry, which supervised SAIL, had been searching for someone who would buy IISCO. There were no purchasers. I discussed the matter fully with Santosh Mohan Dev, then Minister of Steel, and outlined the two conditions basic to my takeover of operations: the choice of technology for modernization would be entirely mine, and I agreed not to terminate the employment of any workers without their consent. We came to an understanding. Dev urged the need for quick action because of the deteriorating situation at IISCO.

However, when final negotiations were going on, the goalposts began to move. SAIL insisted that they should choose the technology required for improvement of IISCO. This, of course, was not acceptable to me. Technology was the key to future progress and I had to be sure that I could freely select the most modern at the most economical price. I did not want to be constricted by government procedures or the problems that inevitably arise when the government gets involved in large purchases. SAIL was not prepared for this. It became apparent that they really were unwilling to give up control. So, I withdrew. Six years later, IISCO's unending losses continue to be a huge burden on the public exchequer. Nothing has changed.

*

Between 1992 and 1994, another interesting investment opportunity arose. The Chief Minister of Orissa, Biju Patnaik, was in London and called at my office. He proposed a joint venture between the state government and myself for the purpose of building a steel plant. The idea seemed feasible and Orissa was a good location, but I was wary of the procedural problems and all the red tape that would be involved. Patnaik was immensely enthusiastic. He said that those obstacles would be handled by him and there would be no corruption or pay-offs. From my room, he telephoned the Prime Minister of India and told him about this project. Narasimha Rao welcomed it. We applied for approval to the Foreign Investment

Planning Board and began preparations for the project. In conformity with government regulations, details of any foreign exchange project, including its capital structure, have to be authorized by the board. They approved our proposal and agreed to a debt to equity ratio of 3 : 1. Both the Prime Minister and the Finance Minister, Manmohan Singh, endorsed our efforts. In order to obtain some of our capital, we visited various government-owned financial institutions in Bombay. Biju Patnaik did something most unusual—he accompanied me on these calls.

The obstacles presented by the financial institutions were amazing. They asked a series of irrelevant questions, including a query as to whether this steel would be required in India in 1999. We were making no progress. The Secretary of Steel, Moosa Raza, arranged another session with the institutions. They claimed that our project costs were too high and demanded a debt to equity ratio of 2 : 1. I told them that our technology would be the very best and that we would obtain it at the lowest price possible. Again they demurred. They were so sure that our costs were excessive, I then said that I was prepared to allow them to buy the technology and build the steel plant—if they could save us money by doing so. There was no response. During these discussions it seemed as though some invisible hand was creating new obstacles and delays whenever any progress was made.

Two years went by and we were still wrapped up in these negotiations and procedures. A disproportionate amount of time was being taken. Resources were being devoured on pettyfogging details. There was little to be gained by continuing. An attractive American opportunity, one that could be speedily concluded, was opening in Farrell, Pennsylvania. I decided to cut my losses and get out. The disappointment of Patnaik and others who had worked on the project was saddening, but there was no reasonable path forward. For an international entrepreneur, time is money and the world offers many choices—a fact of economic life to which the Indian system is singularly blind.

*

Two other situations will underline this conclusion. My brother-in-law, M.D. Jindal, was engaged in a joint venture with Maruti Automobiles, a car manufacturer owned by the Indian government and Suzuki Motors of Japan. He told me that Maruti wanted to outsource pressed steel body parts. They were looking for a supplier who would undertake production. Caparo has much technology and know-how in this field. So, in 1994, we signed an agreement with Maruti and began building a plant in Gurgaon, close to their main operating unit and about ten miles from Delhi.

The plant is now in operation and working fairly well. But, it has taken at least three times longer to get going than a comparable effort would have taken in Britain. There has been a long history of frustrations and delays. I sometimes wonder whether this has been worth the trials and tribulations. I can only hope that things will improve in the future. In the meanwhile, my only satisfaction is that I do have an investment in India and it is a going concern.

My most recent Indian effort has been a joint venture with the Bank of Nova Scotia, a major Canadian institution. In 1993, the Government of India indicated that it wanted to expand private sector banking by encouraging foreign banks. The Bank of Nova Scotia and Caparo made preparations to establish a new commercial bank. To ensure compliance with all official guidelines, we called on the Additional Finance Secretary in charge of banking. Ravi Gupta said the government requirement was fourfold: minimum capital of Rs. 100 crores (about 35 million dollars); maximum non-resident Indian shareholding of 40 per cent; maximum foreign shareholding (Bank of Nova Scotia) of 20 per cent; and the balance 40 per cent to be publicly subscribed. I then visited the Finance Minister and Montek Singh Ahluwalia, the Finance Secretary, who both encouraged me to forward an application for approval.

We engaged Arthur Andersen & Company, an international group of accountants and consultants, to prepare our application. This was submitted to the Reserve Bank of India in June 1994. There was silence for several months, despite assurances from the Finance Minister and Finance Secretary that there were no problems. In January 1995, I met with the Governor of the Reserve Bank, C. Rangarajan, and his deputy, D.R. Mehta, in Bombay. There was, they said, a slight hitch. They could not allow the Bank of Nova Scotia to have their own branch offices in India (they then had only one, in Bombay) while also owning a major share in another commercial bank.

I argued that this was not logical, but it made no impact on their position. After further discussions, the Bank of Nova Scotia agreed to close their branch if this stood in the way of our venture.

During these discussions, I had kept the Finance Minister and the Finance Secretary informed. I brought this latest development to their attention. The Finance Minister telephoned the Governor of the Reserve Bank. I was told that we would get approval since Nova Scotia had agreed to the Reserve Bank conditions. Then, quite suddenly, the Reserve Bank changed its position on another issue. They now insisted that the combined shareholding of the Bank of Nova Scotia and Caparo should not exceed 40 per cent, instead of the original 60 per cent. I protested to both the Finance Minister and Rangarajan. Was there, I inquired, some other consideration, apart from the standard regulations, which prevented approval? Both affirmed that there was none. Yet, here too, the odd pattern of shifting barriers which made any constructive momentum difficult led me to suspect that there were other forces at work.

*

All these painful experiences illustrate the barrier which prevents India from moving ahead: excessive government involvement in the economy. The need to get approvals, licences and clearances from ministers, government departments and regulatory agencies is a deadly minefield. Most of these requirements are unnecessary.

It is customary to blame the bureaucracy and the administrative process for the delays, complexities and tedium in getting things done. However, this is largely an unfair accusation. Many senior bureaucrats are knowledgeable, competent and helpful. When there is no influence or constraint, they function quite effectively. In my view, the real problem lies well beyond this—it is the nexus between political power and administrative decision making. This has allowed the development of a shadowy and powerful phalanx which controls and manipulates the system in exchange for favours and for the benefit of favourites.

The tentacles of New Delhi are too long and too many. This is the result of so much discretionary authority vested in ministers and the ministries. It has two consequences: dishonest politicians, operating behind a screen of bureaucracy, make difficulties and put up obstacles until their greed is satisfied; and honest regulators tend to regard every businessman with distrust, an attitude breeding its own self-protective delays. Until these cosy connections, ghostly influences and suspicions are removed, India will not forge ahead. The reforms of recent years have reduced some of the procedural complications, but they have yet to exorcise the system. Only then will there come a change in attitude and atmosphere that brings the foundations of economic dynamism.

In the past two decades, nations much smaller and with fewer resources than India have become significant global competitors. This progress has brought great benefits to their people. It is well within India's reach to do the same. India's large population, conventionally seen as a liability, is an asset—if the wheels of growth begin to turn. In this context, there are three groups of economic players in India today: a very small number of truly internationally competitive businesses; a significant number of protected industries whose prosperity is artificial because of coddled conditions; and the poor masses yearning for release from poverty and unemployment. This impoverished multitude cannot be liberated until the economy itself is fully liberated. Then, I believe, the natural talent and potential of the Indian people will thrust the country into its proper position in the world and give its people a decent living. The question is, when will we find rulers with the courage and vision to break the caging restrictions, the patronage network and the neomonopolies that enchain India today?

I am often asked why, after my experiences and my reservations, I continue to take an interest in Indian investment. There are three reasons which motivate me. First, I maintain a hope that things will change, and that enlightened thinking will bring this about. Second, I do have a commitment to the land of my birth and I do want to contribute to its development. Third, I feel that some Indian interests will preserve links between my children and the country of their origin, connections that wear thin with the passage of years. If all the ventures I have discussed had evolved as planned, more than ten thousand jobs would have been created in India; many more thousands would have been enriched and much new technology would now be in service. What is more, this would have drawn substantial international investment into the economy, lowering costs and inducing much greater efficiency. That this did not happen is not of much financial consequence to me, but it is emotionally sorrowful. I think the ordinary people of India, who work so hard for so little, deserve better. So, I still dream. Maybe, some day . . .

9

Retrospect and Prospect

About thirty years ago, around the time I came to live in Britain, I read the autobiography of the philosopher Bertrand Russell. I was profoundly moved by a passage in these memoirs:

> Three passions, simple but overwhelmingly strong, have governed my life: the longing for love, the search for knowledge, and unbearable pity for the suffering of mankind. These passions, like great winds, have blown me hither and thither, in a wayward course, over a deep ocean of anguish, reaching to the very verge of despair.

In many ways, these thoughts resonate with the ideas and ideals that inform the Hindu approach to life. As I reflect upon my own experiences, Russell's musings have a particular affinity. His words describe some of the significant quests and circumstances which have conditioned my emotions and the way I look at things.

I believe that the longing for love is almost universal. Yet, as I have learned, it is also paradoxical. It is joy which should evoke and reinforce love. It does—but not with the same depth of meaning as love born through tragedy. I became aware of this because of our trauma with Ambika.

Her expression of love was so pure and unaffected. Our response was no less sincere. But the power of our love was insufficient to give her the life that she and we wanted. For a time, I thought that this was the failure of love and that not to love was perhaps the way to avoid sorrow. But I soon realized that this is no answer. Love, with all its painful possibilities and ecstatic potential, is a reflection of the human condition. We cannot avoid it and each of us has to learn to deal with it in our own unique way.

From my childhood, I was always intellectually curious. Russell says he sought superior knowledge in order to look into the hearts of men. I have had no such ambitions, nor have I been endowed with the psychological genius necessary to do so. My own experience suggests that the motivations of individuals are often so complex that they themselves rarely comprehend the impulses which drive them. I have sought knowledge as a form of self-expression, as a way of relating to the world in which we live, and as a means of responding to some of the questions that intrigue me.

Much of this quest has been focused on my work. To my mind, work is not just employment or making money. It is a way of engaging in society—a door which opens other doors to fulfilment. Learning about my profession has been learning about the world. This involvement has been enormously enriching because it has taken me into a variety of activities and relationships.

Not all of them have been gratifying, but all have provided opportunities for expanding knowledge. Every experience is an education. In this process, formal schooling is very important, especially today. It can, however, only bring us to the gateway of real knowledge—wisdom. And wisdom cannot be taught, although it can be learned.

Wisdom has as many meanings as there are people who think about it. Some philosophic traditions define it as insight, others as godliness, and still others as a kind of spiritual consciousness. None of these descriptions have fully satisfied me. I have tended to think of wisdom as a form of maturity and balance— an outlook that reaches beyond narrow and sectarian perceptions. Neils Bohr, the great Danish physicist, once said that there were two kinds of truths: trivial truths of which the opposite is obviously false and great truths of which the opposite is also true. This, it seems to me, is an attractive proposition. I do not know whether it touches the fringes of wisdom but it makes for much thought. Reflecting upon these questions has been an important part of my life and I hope it will always continue. Those who cease to think, who cease to learn, have essentially ceased to live.

My parents taught me that compassion is both a virtue and a duty. It is a virtue because those who cannot feel for others surely lack a human dimension;

a duty because it is an obligation we have to society and to ourselves.

The vast majority of humankind lives in and requires social context. Like fish need water in which to survive, people need other people in order to lead a fulfilling life. Compassion is the oxygen of such a system. With it, we have a fair chance of evolving a decent social order; without it, society will be dominated by its strongest, most able and most hard-hearted individuals. Strength, ability and ruthlessness may bring material success. Yet, untempered by compassion, they generate the bitterness and mistrust which eventually creates divided nations and political upheavals. A little generosity and understanding would have spared us some of the brutal episodes of history.

Compassion, to me, is not simply open-ended charity, cheque-book sympathy or bleeding-heart liberalism. It has a moral content, but it is also a way in which we can hold society together and improve ourselves by doing so. This is why my own social philosophy is rooted in a sense of communal participation. I feel that every person must make a contribution to the civic environment in which he or she belongs. It is these deposits, the credits of involvement, which build better nations. Not everyone will contribute equally, but everyone should try in whatever ways they can. Yet, I am not a believer in social accounting—benefits being confined only to the productive members of a community. There will always be those who cannot care for themselves. These are obligations society has to fulfil. In doing so, we must bring those who drop out back to useful citizenship.

I believe that the best economic means by which to do this is an enlightened market system. This is, of course, a far cry from the rapacious capitalism that has given enterprise a bad name. My choice is social free enterprise—a fair and responsible way of trying to ensure that every individual can make a good living, get opportunities for self-improvement and have the freedom to realize it in a manner appropriate to his or her capacities. If this involves a certain redistribution of wealth, so be it. But the state must not enforce what its people cannot endure or what destroys their creativity and individualism. This is, after all, the lesson of the communist experiment. One of the central functions of the state is to encourage diversity, not to promote a monopolistic view of right-thinking!

Steady employment is a fundamental element in providing the stability which underwrites independence of the individual. This is why I am a strong promoter of manufacturing industries. Manufacturing provides more kinds of permanent jobs than many other sectors of an economy. Historically, it was the development of manufacturing which began to move workers out of irregular piecework and semi-feudalistic employments. As it expanded, regular payment of workers and an acceptance of their rights took place. The dignity of labour was built on this plinth.

In the 1970s and 1980s it was fashionable to decry manufacturing. Economists, social thinkers and many politicians were clambering aboard the services bandwagon—some even asserting that Britain could well do without manufacturing! I have always resisted these concepts. If something is wrong with our industry, let us fix it. Let us become more competitive. Let us reach for new ways of doing things and for new markets. But, let us not throw out the baby with the bathwater!

In my own way I have tried hard to restore faith in manufacturing industries—and that is basically what the Caparo story is all about. It was a hard struggle, but we were able to demonstrate to ourselves and to others that this is possible when labour and managements work together. This approach was endorsed, in her early years, by Prime Minister Margaret Thatcher and her demand for equal accountability from both unions and management then helped to restore competitiveness to British industry. So, it was somewhat gratifying when Prime Minister John Major, who has been kind and courteous to me, joined in Caparo's twenty-fifth anniversary celebrations in 1994. On that occasion, he acknowledged our efforts in the revival of British industry. I felt a special pride. A business begun by an immigrant was at the cutting edge of a movement to renew an old and neglected economic sector in his adopted homeland.

*

For the past thirty years, almost one-half of my life, I have lived and worked in Britain. I am, then, a child of two cultures—one of birth and the other of choice. It is my good fortune that I am comfortable in both and have never felt displaced in either. India gives me my values and heritage; Britain has given me opportunities to freely express myself. And I am thankful for this. Not many traditional societies allow strangers to make good in their own backyards.

Sometimes, however, such cross-cultural relations lead to amusing interactions. I remember how, in 1978, Lord Mountbatten was preparing his obituary. Of course, Mountbatten had no idea of how soon his tragic end would arrive. However, as a man of precision and detail, he wanted to be sure that his death notices would cover all facets of his career—including his tenure as the last Viceroy of India. Hearing that Jagjivan Ram, then Deputy Prime Minister of India, was visiting London, Mountbatten asked me to arrange for Ram to be interviewed in anticipation of his (Mountbatten's) demise. The former Viceroy did not know that talking about death is anathema to elderly South Asians. But Ram did! When I told him of the request, he exploded: 'Mountbatten has gone mad. So have you. Do you think I am also mad to discuss a living person's death?'

There are those who talk of racism in Britain today. They are not wrong. But it is useful to remember that such repugnant attitudes afflict only a small segment of the population. Unfortunately, most societies do have forms of discrimination directed against outsiders. In this context, it is remarkable how generally tolerant the British are about the multi-cultural transformation of their country in so short a period. The character of Britain has changed dramatically in recent years. Many old taboos have fallen or are giving way. The adjustment process is not easy and, inevitably, stresses and tensions arise. However, one of the really redeeming features is that there are always many native Britons who are prepared to fight for fairness to immigrants and foreigners.

All of us who have joined this society have a commitment to make the new Britain work. Most migrants have come voluntarily and this is now our home. There are currently well over two million persons of Asian origin living here and they have made an outstanding contribution. We are a highly productive group and our reputation for hard work and diligence has been justly earned. The community has low crime and welfare rates. Most of its children are well educated. Gradually, more individuals of Asian background are participating in public activities and the number of those elected to public office has increased significantly. Yet, we still are able to keep many of our traditions. Family life remains the core of our social structure.

However, there remains among many of us, especially those who were born in India, a tendency to be socially introverted. None of us can or should ever forget that India is our motherland, but we must recognize that Britain is now our homeland. It is not necessary to import and sustain differences from India. These are not the lessons we should be teaching our children. They should begin to realize that the things which unite us are so much more than those which divide us. In fact, those of my generation have something to learn from younger Indo-Brits today— they are far more open to cross-cultural experiences and integrations than we are. Some seniors regret this. I think it is unavoidable and these are early signs of an emerging role for the community in the mainstream of British life.

Of course, many older Asians are disturbed when our young people act differently, dress differently, relax differently and speak differently from their parents. But they should remind themselves that it is we who brought them here and exposed them to education, culture and recreation in this environment. In such circumstances, must we seek clones of ourselves? The best we can and should expect is that our youth be good and caring citizens. When a generation past seeks to impose its attitudes and norms on a generation present it only provokes resentment and rebellion.

To me, it is sufficient to pass on the values I hold dear—and the chances of their acceptance are much greater if our progeny come to them through their own understanding rather than through our preachings.

*

These ideas and approaches eventually led me to participate in the activities of the Labour Party. In the mid-1970s, I came to know Michael and Jill Foot. Michael was then an important figure in the party, soon to become its leader. He encouraged my interest in Labour and was the godfather of an affiliation that has increasingly engaged me during the past twenty years. This has been an era of ups and downs for the party—perhaps the most traumatic period of its existence. But those of us who have been consistent in our support never doubted that a stronger organization would emerge from all these tribulations.

The Labour Party has been a congenial ideological

home for me because its bedrock philosophy addresses social justice. Having lived my youth in Gandhi's India, this ethic has a special appeal. The ideals of fairness to all communities and special concern for the underprivileged was part of the political air we breathed. Gandhi taught us that colonialism was bad, but that the colonialism within societies was even worse. These notions, together with my gratitude for Labour's anti-imperial record in South Asia, made me feel I belonged in the party.

In the past decades or so, the evolution of Labour's economic philosophy has strengthened my belief that this is a party capable of change and of changing society for the better.

In the course of my association with Labour, I came to know its four most recent leaders—and have been fortunate to know them as personal friends. Although very unlike each other in personality and style, they have all had rich qualities of heart and mind. Only one of them has become Prime Minister, but all would have been inspiring heads of government in their time. Michael Foot is an intellectual giant whose gifts match his passionate political commitments. I have learned a lot from him and, over the years, Michael and his wife Jill have been a singular source of encouragement. His interest in India long preceded our friendship, but it helped to bring us closer. At a celebration of his seventy-fifth birthday, I was able to express some of these sentiments:

> History has a special place for good people in public life. This has nothing to do with success or

failure, victory or defeat. It is a place for those who
have rare virtues and values—loyalty, commitment,
sincerity, wisdom and justice. Michael will rank
high among these saints of civic endeavour . . .
Many think of Michael as an idealist—the last
political romantic. But he is also a realist. The
advice he has often given me has been sound and
practical . . .

It was through Michael and Jill that I was introduced
to Neil Kinnock, whom they had recognized early as
a potential leader. Neil is a man of courage and great
warmth. With determination and moderation, he
guided Labour for a decade and made the party
much more acceptable to the average voter. One of
his most endearing qualities is his faith in ordinary
people and his humanity. After Neil's resignation as
Leader of the Labour Party, I invited him to be an
adviser to the Caparo Group. He was a wise and
helpful counsellor until he moved on to the European
Commission.

John Smith who succeeded was truly Britain's lost
leader. Few individuals in politics have had his honesty
and his dedication. Just as he was coming into his
own, illness struck John down (he died of a heart
attack on 12 May 1994) and deprived the country of
a strong, fair-minded and forthright captain. As a
newspaper headline then put it: 'John Smith was the
best Prime Minister Britain never had.' How strange
are the ways of fate—sometimes raising persons to
the brink of greatness and then ending it all. John's
destiny is a warning that uncertainty stalks everyone
and the unknown is a trapdoor through which anyone
can fall.

The workings of politics have changed remarkably in modern times and the requirements for leaders have transformed accordingly. Organization, systems, management and media skills are critically important.

The demands on a leader are now much more complex than ever before—so much so that some of the greatest figures from the past would probably not do very well in the present environment! Fortunately, in Tony Blair, we have a leader who understands the new politics and yet retains an inspirational flair for motivating others. Tony is still in the early stage of his stewardship. His proven capacity for personal growth suggests that he will be an outstanding prime minister.

I once asked Indira Gandhi what was the single most important quality a prime minister needed. Her answer: 'The capacity to say "no" and to stick with your decision.' Tony Blair has that ability and something more—a turn of mind that is always searching for creative answers to what are often intractable questions. So, I have a lot of confidence in his future. But I also have a concern: the expectations of the new Prime Minister are so high that no mortal will be able to fulfil them. When the honeymoon ends, Tony will face many trials—some of which will be as unfair as they can be. Then, his fortitude will be tested to the full. I know he has the inner stamina to face these tides, but I hope he will not be discouraged as decent men tend to be when confronted with the meanness of political life today.

In the upper echelons of the Labour Party are many of exceptional talent. This is testimony to the party's ability to attract the best and the brightest even in years of adversity. Among them are Gordon Brown and Robin Cook.

Gordon is a man of vision whose intellectual abilities are supplemented with an ingredient essential for success at the Exchequer: he is performance oriented. What is more, he has three qualities that I have not often seen combined in any statesman—an extraordinary appetite for work, a constant desire to do what is right for the country and a willingness to learn. Gordon is both tough-minded and sensitive, a mix not easy to reconcile. My respect for his personal integrity has only increased as I have got to know him better and to appreciate his character.

In late 1996, I accompanied Robin Cook, then shadow foreign secretary, on an official visit to India. We had discussions with a variety of individuals and groups. I was immensely impressed by the way in which Robin handled intricate issues. His diplomatic finesse and acumen suggest that his tenure in the Foreign Office will be very fruitful. What makes him unusual is an informality and refreshing readiness to listen. The universe of diplomacy can do with this approach. It has become far too stuffy and protocol conscious, thereby divorcing it from the real world. Such detachment is dangerous because foreign policy loses its credibility when it does not connect to domestic affairs. Robin Cook knows this better than many foreign ministers I have met. Since he blends nationalism and internationalism, he will be able to define British interests while maintaining larger humanitarian imperatives.

*

In the summer of 1996, I heard rumours that my name was to be submitted for a peerage. I did not pay much attention until I learned that the Leader of the Opposition (Tony Blair) had recommended this to Prime Minister John Major. With the Prime Minister's approval, a list of proposed new peers is then forwarded to the Queen. On the morning of 6 August 1996, when I was in my office working on this manuscript, I received the following letter:

10 DOWNING STREET
LONDON SW1A 2AA

THE PRIME MINISTER   5 August 1996
    IN CONFIDENCE

Dear Swraj,

I am writing to let you know, in strict confidence, that I shall shortly be recommending to The Queen the creation of a number of Life Peers in a special list to increase the working strength of the House of Lords.

I have it in mind to submit your name to The Queen with a recommendation that Her Majesty may be graciously pleased to approve that the dignity of a Barony of the United Kingdom for Life be conferred upon you.

I hope that you will be able to let me know as soon as possible that this would be agreeable to you.

Yours Sincerely
John Major

Once the usual formalities were completed, a public announcement was made on 21 August 1996. I was then away on holiday, but when I returned the response was overwhelming. Good wishes, cards, telegrams and flowers flowed in from all parts of the world. My office was swamped with over ten thousand messages of congratulation. The telephone literally never stopped ringing. A large number of letters and notes came from people in Britain and India whom I did not know—just ordinary people, many of them in modest circumstances, who somehow identified with my appointment to the House of Lords. I was both excited and humbled by this outpouring, deeply touched that so many saw my peerage as somehow symbolic of their own aspirations and moved by the affectionate nature of their greetings.

On 12 November 1996 I was introduced to the House of Lords. It is usual to take a title. Since most peers adopt the name of the area in which they reside, I chose the designation Lord Paul of Marylebone in the City of Westminster. The introduction is a solemn ceremony, when the new peer, attired in his regalia and robes, is presented by two sponsors. Mine were Lord Haskel, an old friend, and the Baroness Smith, widow of John Smith. As I walked into the House, accompanied by them and watched from the gallery by my family and close friends, I could scarcely control my emotions. Tears welled up and it was with forced restraint that I managed to go through the oath of allegiance.

My thoughts flooded with distant and random memories. How surprised and happy my parents would have been to see the closing of the circle—the son of

a family of freedom fighters being admitted to an
assembly where so much of Indian history has been
decided. If only my darling Ambika had been able to
watch all this—perhaps she did from wherever she is.
I knew my brothers in India, Jit and Stya, shared my
feelings, but I missed the good humour of our
deceased sibling, Surrendra. He would have had a
joke to make or a story to tell about the Lord Swraj!
There were so many others who were not there, and
to them I owed so much. Suddenly, there came to
mind an incident which happened in New Delhi in
1983. The then President of India, Giani Zail Singh,
held a reception for the visiting Queen of England.
Quite unexpectedly, he beckoned to me and
introduced me to Her Majesty, saying: 'Swraj is India's
gift to Britain!' Preceding the introduction, there was
a luncheon in the Lords Cholmondeley Room. Many
nice things were said and done. Yet, throughout the
camaraderie and cordiality, I felt a lingering sadness.
Those with whom I most wanted to share these
moments would never know of them.

The House of Lords is an institution in which
members can participate as much or as little as they
wish. There are about one thousand hereditary and
life peers, but regular attendees number around three
hundred or so. These 'working' lords sustain the
business of a second legislative chamber and conduct
a substantial amount of parliamentary work. I resolved
to actively engage in the proceedings of the House.
This means that I am fully affiliated with the Labour
Parliamentary Group and sit on the party benches.
To my mind, membership implies certain obligations

and I see no purpose in being a peer for titular or ornamental reasons.

A new peer can make his or her maiden speech at any time. Some take months or even years to do so; others have a greater sense of urgency. Soon, I made my first address. In this initial statement it is customary to present oneself to the House before focusing on the specific topic on the agenda. As I rose to speak, the significance of the surroundings seemed to reach out to me. These panelled walls and red leather benches have witnessed the march of history. Here, great debates have taken place and celebrated orators waxed eloquent. During World War II, when their own hall was destroyed, the House of Commons met in this chamber and it was then that Winston Churchill delivered his stirring speeches. Inspired by these thoughts, I tried to put my own feelings into words.

Maiden Speech, House of Lords
Thursday 28 November 1996

My Lords,
It was just sixteen days ago that I was introduced to Your Lordships' House. However, the courtesy and kindness which Your Lordships have shown me in this brief period encourages me to speak today. My Lords, I come to this House conscious that the roots of my heritage and philosophy are not conventional to the membership of this august assembly. Yet, I believe Your Lordships recognize that they symbolize a contribution to the new Britain which we are all engaged in constructing. There was a time when the strength of nations was measured by exclusion and exclusivity. Today, My

Lords, we heed a larger truth—that there is more strength in diversity, more vigour in variety.

At this moment, I am also mindful that my presence among Your Lordships signifies another convergence—the reconciliation and friendship between the land of my birth and the country which is my home. The underlying spirit in which Britain and India now relate to each other is a model for the world.

In its own modest way, my personal history reflects this. My family, who were ardent participants in India's independence movement, named me Swraj for their ideals of freedom and self-rule. Swraj means freedom—the eternal cry that resonated in my youth. However, had I known that one day I would have to address Your Lordships and this House, I would have wished to be named 'Fearless'.

After university in India, I continued higher studies at the Massachusetts Institute of Technology in the United States. At MIT, I learned much about engineering and much more about life. The two great things it taught me were to always aspire for excellence and to never abandon hope.

Thirty years ago, I came to this country in search of medical treatment for my daughter whom we later, sadly, lost. For a while, I did abandon hope. But that tragic beginning unfolded into a new life and a successful career largely because of the opportunities which Britain provides. These opportunities, leavened with the support which hard work and determination still receive in this country, enabled me to revive industries which were largely abandoned or downgraded some decades ago. Britain is a country where responsible citizenship earns many rewards. Whatever pressures arise, let us not close our doors to those who bring their skills to these shores.

My Lords, our attention today focuses upon the Budget which Her Majesty's Government has presented. Because of my long association with manufacturing industry, I am especially concerned with those components of the Budget that address this sector of our economy. I believe that, in recent years, manufacturing industry has received less recognition than it deserves. For me, manufacturing is the bedrock of the British economy. It is what first provided stable and permanent employment to the masses in this country and in this part of the world—and it still does.

This is why I am disappointed that the Budget has not given any specific encouragement to the need for capital investment in industry. Britain's manufacturing base is at a critical stage in its history. There has been a prolonged erosion of this plinth on which our economy stands. The principal components of industrial competitiveness need to be re-examined and their requirements re-assessed. Capital investment has been limited, and this has inhibited the acquisition of modern technology. We have to find ways to increase capital inputs and so to upgrade plants and facilities. Today, we risk falling behind Western Europe and Asia Pacific—not only because our skills are inadequate but because our equipment needs modernization.

Ours is not human failure. During the past

decade or so, some of our shopfloor managements and workforces have demonstrated competence and achieved levels of productivity comparable to that of any economy. But their reputation for innovation and quality cannot be maintained without high technology.

Another issue close to my heart is that entrepreneurial businesses—the small and medium size companies which were once the pace-setters of industrial Britain—are now losing ground. While publicly quoted companies find it relatively easy to raise capital, it is much harder for privately owned businesses. The financial community, and those who make financial policy, should look at private companies in a different light because it is these businesses that are often the source of industrial innovation. In the investment climate which now prevails, it is easier to raise capital for football clubs than for industrial ventures. This is cutting the lifeline of some of the potentially best and brightest British firms. High-flying financial engineering may be the trapeze artistry of the commercial world, but the small entrepreneur forms the safety net of society. The human and social costs of industrial neglect will soon come to haunt us unless we move rapidly to reinforce and renovate the most basic parts of our economy.

We must enthuse a younger generation about the benefits and excitement of an industrial career. We must develop an approach that looks forward to the time when British manufactures will evoke the respect they once enjoyed in global markets. Given our traditional talents, it is surely not difficult to elevate our industries to world-class excellence.

But we can never achieve this with policies of indifference.

My Lords, I have worked on the shop floor and I have managed large enterprises. I know the hope which a growing industrial economy brings to working men and women. We have an obligation to rekindle these hopes because I passionately believe that what is good for British industry is good for Britain.

The House of Lords is a serious assembly. There is none of the cross-talk, interjection or sharp retort which so enlivens the proceedings in the House of Commons. Relations between members are friendly and not at all partisan. The peers who participate frequently maintain a high level of discussion in a calm atmosphere. Whenever the House is in session, I attend regularly and speak in debates. Committees sit often. Parliamentary life and work interests me much more than I had expected—a new career which I am beginning to enjoy.

*

By early 1997, everyone was aware that another General Election was coming. The Conservative government had run its full term. Election fever began to mount. Labour was generally favoured to win but nobody expected it to be an easy victory. All political groups began preparing for the final countdown. At last, the date of the election was fixed: 1st May.

All of us were kept very busy. I campaigned

wherever I was asked to go. There were two constituencies which I was particularly active in canvassing—the business community and the South Asian community. My message to business was simply that Labour was entrepreneur-friendly and very supportive of free enterprise. As a businessman, I knew this to be true and any propaganda to the contrary was scare tactics by our opponents. From the reactions I received it was evident that the many reassurances already given by Tony Blair and Gordon Brown had been accepted. Most company executives were no longer in the Tory camp. Of South Asians, I asked just one question: Which party do you think will protect your interests better and provide more opportunities for your children? There was little else that had to be said.

As Election Day neared, the contrast between the two main forces was marked. The policy differences were not so great as they had once been, signalling the fact that, for the most part, Britain is a nation which has achieved a consensus on its social and economic goals. But Labour presented a dynamic and fresh outlook while the Tories appeared tired and bereft of ideas. After eighteen years in office, it was time to go. Towards the end, the Tory effort was undermined by sharp internal divisions and had an air of desperation about it. The Labour team functioned smoothly and Tony Blair proved to be a star on the hustings.

In the early evening of election night, 1st May, Aruna and I drove to Hampstead. Our old friends Michael and Jill Foot were hosting a party together with Melvyn Bragg and Cate Haste, the literary and media personalities. All the guests were Labour supporters. The mood was cheerful as the election results began to come in on television sets put up in three rooms. Exit polls proclaimed that Labour would have a strong lead. This received a big cheer, but there was still some apprehension that these projections might be overstated.

From Hampstead we moved on to the BBC Television studios, where guests from all political parties were attending a large gathering. By this time, the actual results were beginning to come through. In the initial sixty seats that were declared there was not a single Conservative victory.

The friends of Labour were jubilant. It was clear that a big sweep was in the making. The Conservatives who were present looked very downcast. Many of them had expected a defeat but not one so drastic.

Leaving the BBC, we proceeded to the Royal Festival Hall. This was an official function organized by the Labour Party to thank its workers. It became a lively celebration. By the time we reached there over one hundred and fifty results had been announced. The Labour lead was growing bigger and bigger. There was a sense of excitement but also of anticipation—everyone was awaiting the Labour total to reach an absolute majority. Finally, at about 2.45 a.m., the news came. The Labour count had reached 330 seats and the party would form the next government. There was an explosion of resounding cheers. As we got information on the defeat of various Conservative leaders, the shouts broke out again. It was heartening to watch the enthusiasm. Many Labourites were too young to remember previous victories. For them, it was a wholly new experience and they relished it.

The architects of the triumph began to arrive. Everyone was delighted to see the former leader, Neil Kinnock, and the affection in which he is still held was evident. At 4.00 a.m. Gordon Brown and Robin Cook entered to a tremendous welcome.

Shortly thereafter, at 4.15 a.m., Tony Blair came in to another tumultuous reception. He had flown in from his constituency in Durham and looked every bit the Prime Minister to be. The applause was so loud and prolonged that his speech was almost drowned by the noise.

This was really an evening to cherish. The joy of the event washed away, at least for the moment, the pain and struggles of the path to victory. Few gave thought to the tasks of administration ahead. That was for tomorrow. After eighteen years, Labour was back—and everyone wanted to bask in the glory of the moment. It was Labour's finest hour in quite a while. That night, we enjoyed it to the full.

*

In early July each year, Aruna and I host an afternoon reception at the Ambika Paul Children's Zoo in Regent's Park, London. It is an occasion when hundreds of our friends and their children come to enjoy the attractive surroundings and the convivial atmosphere. This is also an annual remembrance for

Ambika, in whose name I helped to restore the zoo. An elegant statue, set in a fountain, serves as a permanent memorial to her.

Our 1997 gathering was particularly significant. I had been elevated to the House of Lords, Caparo was prospering after the first year of management by my three sons, the Labour Party was back in government, and India was about to commemorate fifty years of independence. Neither good times nor lean times endure forever. But, with God's grace, this was a pleasing moment.

There was another reason which made it all the more special. Aruna and I celebrated forty years of marriage. During these four decades we have shared joys and tragedy. Through it all, Aruna's patience, encouragement and good humour sustained me. She has brought me extraordinary happiness and whatever I achieved has been built on the stability of the home we have made together. I have been fortunate in that my family life has given me the strength to bear burdens and the emotional resources so necessary for success.

I resolved to make a small public acknowledgement of my debt to Aruna. Unknown to her, I arranged with the London Zoo to construct a new enclosure in her honour. The officials of the zoo felt that the addition of a pygmy hippopotamus pen would add something unique. These are a rare African species on the verge of extinction. To breed them would perhaps help to rescue these animals. We went to work in secrecy, constructing the enclosure and securing a pair of the pygmy hippos. Aruna had no knowledge of this.

Imagine her surprise when a plaque was unveiled giving her name to this section of the zoo. And this was most appropriate because Aruna is herself the rarest of persons! The plaque reads:

London Zoo
"Hippo Wallow"
The Baroness Paul Pygmy Hippo Enclosure
Dedicated to
Aruna Paul
in celebration of forty years of marriage (1956–1996)
and with gratitude for constant love,
caring and support of our family
from
Swraj, children and grandchildren
29 June 1997
The Ambika Paul Foundation
Caparo Group Limited

*

As I look back on my own life and on the lives of others, it seems as if everyone's existence is circumscribed by boundaries. These are the limits which are set for us by society and by the situations in which we find ourselves. Some individuals seek happiness by living within these limits. If that is their inclination they are right to do so. Few can make a good life by constantly resisting their instincts. Yet, for others, reaching beyond the horizon is part of their nature. They should not deny it.

I have always looked upon boundaries as challenges. Sometimes, this approach got me into trouble. But I believe that what really makes us human is the ambition to test limits and to quest beyond the conventional. To me, endeavour is fulfilment—whatever the results may be. I hope life will allow me to do this until the end comes, and to do it in my own way.

Long years ago, a clever young student questioned his teacher: 'Guruji, for many decades you have tried to change the world. You exhaust yourself in doing this. Even now, in old age, you keep on struggling to change the world. You are a wise man and surely you know that you cannot achieve this. Why do you continue such a foolish effort—you will never change the world.' The sage looked sadly at his pupil: 'My son, you suffer from the exuberant expectations of youth. Why do I continue? Of course I know I cannot change the world, but I continue because I don't want the world to change me!'

Appendices

During the past two decades, I have been invited to address many public gatherings, conferences, meetings and seminars. Such occasions have provided opportunities to express my philosophy, ideas and sentiments about a variety of subjects. Excerpts from these speeches have been selected and arranged by Elizabeth Allan, my executive assistant for almost twenty years. Her diligence in this and other matters has been far beyond the call of duty. I am deeply appreciative of her helpfulness.

Appendix I

INDIA

Heritage and Traditions

The Indian tradition has always embraced the idea of global vision. Our ancient sages imparted wisdom that Indians absorbed, but it was also wisdom for the world. They encouraged our forefathers, and us, to think in broad perspectives—the view of universalism. Our great leaders of more modern times—Mahatma Gandhi, Jawaharlal Nehru, Rabindranath Tagore, Sarojini Naidu, Indira Gandhi and others—taught us that nationalism must go hand in hand with internationalism. It is true that many of our people were, and are, parochial, but our tradition is not. And, since Independence in 1947, successive Indian governments have manifested this tradition in world affairs.

Massachusetts Institute of Technology
25 April 1987

The philosophic tradition which has shaped my own perspectives is Hinduism. The vital spiritual scriptures of Hinduism—the Vedas, the Upanishads and, above all, the Celestial Song of the Lord Krishna (the Bhagavad Gita)— all tell us the need to balance the conquest of outer space with the conquest of the inner space within us. From the wellspring of Hinduism came other profound philosophies and ethical systems, such as Buddhism. They brought India's message to the world: There is an interconnectedness of time and space—and we ignore it at our peril.

American College of Switzerland, Leysin
10 May 1985

Indian values and culture is the seedbed from which most of us have come. The most enduring roots of Indian tradition are lodged in the family. To many in modern society, family values and family relationships seem outdated today. Yet, to us who have an association with Indian society, the family still means much. What do family values mean? They mean, essentially, two things. One learns a sense of caring about others and about their problems and concerns. We also learn that each individual can only work as part of a larger unit, and that successful cooperation comes from teamwork.

London School of Economics
11 March 1987

Those of us with a Bengali background who live abroad are forced to think of Bengal as two worlds—the world of reality and the world of image. The world of reality is what we know Bengal to be. Where else can you find such a blend of culture and rationality; where else are people so concerned with life and with the life of the mind? We

know how true it is when Calcutta is called the City of
Soul.

Bengal Initiative, Calcutta
29 December 1995

Indian social values have a resonance with our era. At the
heart of our social structure is the family. Although there
has been some erosion in our concept of family ties,
relatives and family still have a special meaning for us. We
ourselves must re-affirm our own commitment to the
family as an institution. If we lose our family awareness, we
have lost a very important part of our tradition and much
of what we have to offer other societies. For us, in
particular, children are our wealth in a much more than
material sense. As Gurudev Rabindranath Tagore once
said: 'Every child comes with the message that God is not
yet discouraged of man.' If this sentiment is universalized,
most of the world's troubles will be resolved.

Non-Resident Indians Convention, Delhi
20 December 1995

Each society, each individual evolved answers to the great
questions of life. My own roots are lodged in the
philosophic heritage of India. So, I naturally turn to those
sources of information which inform my tradition. From
the ancient classics of the Vedas and the Bhagavad Gita,
through the teachings of the Buddha to Mahatma Gandhi,
a powerful message resonates: The quest and the spirit of
the quest is as significant as the result. The eternal questions
often arise, as these things do, in the midst of the most
mundane activities and in the most ordinary course of life.
As we grapple with our responses, we must never be
discouraged. We may not be able to fully answer these
questions, but it is perhaps more important to question

our answers—our ways of approaching them—and to keep trying.

Chapman University, California
26 May 1995

Indian Society Today

India is a nation of two worlds. In one, modern maharajas maintain standards of living and methods of operation that are reminiscent of feudal privilege. In the other, the masses struggle for a better life and a better India. To narrow this gap will take time and courage. It will take great efforts to instil values of corporate and social morality in the maharajas of today. It will take much earnest struggle to move the masses forward. Yet, unless both are done together, India cannot succeed in the future.

Indian Community Forum, Los Angeles
27 July 1985

Today we are in danger of becoming a nation without too many people of character. In many walks of life you see too many people who are willing to sell themselves for money or position. The greatest danger to our country is not from outside attack, from mismanagement, or even from the ravages of nature. It is from a growing moral decay—a lack of character. People who get and give bribes, those who have no principles, those who will do anything to get ahead—these are the real enemies of our country and our tradition. It is often the lamp inside which burns down the house.

Apeejay Schools Prize Convocation, Delhi
23 December 1988

Ancient Indian society valued the family so much. Now, quite suddenly, in a generation or two, the family is breaking up and societies are breaking up. Let us not blame anyone for this except ourselves. For instance, if we do not care how our children conduct themselves, if we do not spend enough time with them, who is to blame? If we want to progress, we have to restore family structure and values. There is no use referring to Western examples and answers. Even Indian individualism flourishes best when it is rooted in the family system. After all, modernization does not always mean Westernization. I think we can learn something here from the Japanese and how they retain their social structure while transforming their economy.

The great sages of the Indian past discussed the concept of Vasudaiva Kutumbakam—the world is a whole, the essential unity of perspective. Now, I am no great philosopher or pundit, but I know this—Vasudaiva Kutumbakam is the most appropriate organizing principle of modern economics and modern business. No international business can function today except on this principle. Surely then, we can apply a little of this to our own society. After much experience, I have come to believe that great things are often achieved not by vast and instant changes but by incremental steps. Ten per cent more unity and ten per cent less greed and India will be a major world power.

Rotary Club, Calcutta
27 December 1994

It is eight years since I last had the pleasure of addressing your group. In this time, a century of history has happened in India and around the world. Changes we could not have dreamed of have taken place. I often wonder whether we have learned from these experiences and these events. Are we any wiser? Have we reflected enough upon the meaning of these changes? Or do the words of the French proverb apply: The more things change, the more they are the same? The most evident feature that strikes any Indian abroad, looking at his motherland, is the recent growth of terrorism. The toll of terrorism has deprived the country of two of its leaders. But the horror at great events about big people should not conceal concern at the fate of lesser known people. No Indian should be insensitive to the death by terrorism of thousands of ordinary citizens in recent years. I only hope that those in authority will be sensitive to these never-ending and dreadful tragedies. Yet, terrorism is not only political. Economic terrorism has wounded the country also. What is economic terrorism? It is mismanagement, corruption, maladministration, favouritism and any other action that destroys our economy and its potential. There is no other name for it. Destruction of our economy destroys the hopes and aspirations of ordinary people. It destroys their faith in democracy. It destroys their future.

Indian Journalists Forum, Delhi
30 August 1991

Unfortunately the present status of India encourages a few people to become very rich and lead a cosseted, protected lifestyle. This does not do anything for the masses of people who still live below the poverty line. Sooner, rather than later, we must ensure that these people too enjoy the fruits of a prosperous and industrialized community. Otherwise freedom will have no meaning to them and they will rally to demagogic messages put forth by unscrupulous rabble-rousers. And then, the edifice of our democracy will tumble.

Non-Resident Indians Institute, Delhi
26 December 1991

In India today all our attention and focus has been on economic liberalization and on the middle class in India.

We tend to forget that all these reforms, all these foreign investments, all this talk of progress, affects only a small part of India. There is still a huge underclass—the rural poor, the urban destitute and displaced—who are untouched by all this talk and all the policy changes. If something is not done for them, we are sitting on a time bomb! The tragic earthquake in Maharashtra will be nothing compared to this earthquake if it takes place. Let us not be deceived by the context of our world. There is another world out there—a world whose needs must be addressed if we are to avoid a war between these two groups.

Non-Resident Indians Institute, Delhi
26 December 1991

Corruption is a social cancer. What is the use of our taking pride in our moral traditions and philosophic heritages if our modern tradition and modern philosophy is to take it when you can make it? The prevalence of corruption is the greatest deterrent to economic improvement. This is a particular challenge to all of us today. We can reform our economy day and night, but if progress is not made in reducing corruption, most of our gains will be eroded.

Bengal Chamber of Commerce
27 December 1994

My message has been a simple one: until, and unless, we in India end economic discrimination, provide opportunity for ability, and learn to play by rules that are fair for all, we will be a divided and backward nation. This is the truth about our business world, about the world of politics, about our society. Forty years ago, India was born out of the concept of equality of opportunity. This is what our great leaders—Mahatma Gandhi, Jawaharlal Nehru and

Indira Gandhi—stood for and worked for. Yet today, in almost every area of society, we have an unacceptable level of discrimination, and equality of opportunity is a myth.

Lions Club, Calcutta
29 December 1988

The democratic process is firmly established in India. Whenever Indians are frustrated or angered by government they make their displeasure felt through the democratic process. The threat of dictatorship, always a factor in many developing countries, is extremely remote in India. Whatever shortcomings exist, a vibrant civil society tries hard to address matters like human rights and environmental degradation. At a time when the key question about emerging nations is not so much their promise as their stability, India ranks high.

Thornton Asia Conference, London
8 March 1995

India's Economy/Economic Reforms

The economic experience of modern India indicates that two constraints retarded our progress. The first was the system as it evolved. The global economic world in which we lived advanced to new levels of sophistication and more productive ways of organizing investment and production. In contrast, our policy makers believed that a regulated, restricted and largely closed market was of great benefit to India. Actually, it was only of great benefit to a very few. Ironically, state socialism proved more beneficial to the economic elite than any form of competitive capitalism. Urgent reforms were needlessly delayed and this delay has caused untold misery to hundreds of millions of Indians. I hope somebody will take responsibility for this. In fact, some may well ask whether there was a plan by self-serving interests to avoid or postpone economic reforms in order to fill their pockets. Anyway, the lesson is clear—we must never again allow ourselves to be misled in this way!

Bengal Chamber of Commerce
27 December 1994

There is, and will always be, some tension between international business and local nationalism. We also understand that governments come and go. As we have seen in Eastern Europe, no political structure, however strong it may appear, is immune from sudden upheaval. Things change, and sometimes that is necessary. Yet, this is where India scores. Whatever politics may bring, the constitutional framework provides a stability that few other countries have.

Bengal Initiative, Calcutta
29 December 1995

Indian exports in 1993 were around 20 billion dollars. Japan exported over 350 billion dollars, South Korea about 90 billion dollars and even tiny Taiwan exported 90 billion dollars. Malaysia and Thailand each exported about twice as much as India in 1993. India accounts for only about one-half of one per cent of total world exports today. If we want to develop the national economy we have to increase this paltry figure and do it fast.

Delhi University
21 December 1994

Between the Central Mediterranean and the East Pacific, India is the only country which has all the ingredients for becoming a major economic force in the near future. Such an ambition is a noble one only if it is built on a foundation of broad-based prosperity—otherwise it is a shaky pyramid. Such an objective is well within our reach— if we can put some of our house in order. The economic reforms offer us that chance. This is the time to seize it. The moment is near when critical economic policy decisions will have to be made. There are always those who will urge caution and point to the risks and the possible political consequences. To them I will say that the risks and consequences of slowing down are far, far greater than those of going ahead. We have planted some productive seeds in the fertile fields of Indian endeavour. They have sprouted encouragingly. But, before they can grow further and be fully fruitful, a lot more weeding has to be done. Let us get on with the job.

Bengal National Chamber of Commerce
27 December 1994

A major question concerns Indian industrialists who have benefited from sleepy socialist protection and prospered in an atmosphere of noncompetitive inefficiency. These mollycoddled establishmentarians feel threatened by the new order. Instead of becoming more efficient and more competitive, they are becoming more obstructive. Witness the Bombay Club, a strong lobby based on a secret meeting of powerful industrialists in Bombay. Given their influence and financial clout, they are capable of great obstruction—maybe even attempting to change the government. They will buy, bully, or battle to get their way. They may. Yet, I doubt whether they will succeed in the long term.

International Business Club
Northwestern University, Chicago
3 March 1994

The phase of easy reform accomplishments is about to end. From here on the haul will be much tougher. India now has to make serious political choices in the substance and selections of its more difficult reforms. It cannot go much further simply with technocratic fiddling at the margins. The question is: Whether India's politicians and its political system are mature enough and thoughtful enough to make the right choices? Or will they cling to the wrong choices that they have stuck to for far too long.

Citiforum Conference, London
2 May 1995

The innate caution of Congress leadership has prevented reform from going far enough—or fast enough—for the benefits to reach lower income groups. The reverses suffered by the Congress Party in recent years have less to do with reform than with other social and political factors such as communal affairs and corruption. I am convinced that the voters are punishing policy makers, not for the reforms, but for not sharing the benefits of the reforms with the masses. These things aside, there are other reasons why any administration is likely to maintain the reform process. Indian culture is particularly congenial to the type of change which economic reform will bring.

SMI Conference, London
31 January 1996

We are often swept back and forth by waves of opinion. At times, euphoria about India's economic changes make that country look like Ali Baba's cave! On the other hand, there are those who say that the more things change, the more they are the same. Between these surges of optimism and doubt lies an opportunity for all those interested in expanding their investment and trade into the second most populous country in the world. But that opportunity can only be developed if we take a hard, and a hardheaded, look at India.

SMI Conference, London
31 January 1996

A large number of Indians are looking for change. They want a transparent system. They want a fair and competitive environment. This is why I urge foreign investors not to accept quick-fix solutions and not to play by some of the back-door rules. In short, not to succumb to the temptations of the weaknesses of the system as it is. This will only damage the reform process and do a great disservice to the country. It will also taint the whole idea of foreign investment and, ultimately, create more problems for those who engineer such involvements.

Confederation of British Industry
29 April 1996

The public debate [about NRI investment in Indian companies] has tended to focus around the question of non-resident investments. This is only one part of the issue. In fact, the implications of this matter go far beyond. Among other things, they concern:

First : The use and misuse of funds which government institutions hold in trust for the public and invest on its behalf.

Second: They concern the investment of these public funds in public companies, which are controlled by managements who have a limited financial interest in these businesses.

Third : They concern the impropriety of these managements and public accountability for the benefits they have extracted from public companies which they manage like private estates.

Fourth : They concern the impact of the actions of these managements (like refusal to register legally acquired shares) on the financial structure of Indian business—on markets, on stockbrokers, on all owners of shares and other negotiable instruments, on the integrity of investments.

Fifth : They concern the relationship between the overseas Indian community and the Indian business establishment at home.

All India Investors Association, Bombay
6 August 1983

Everyone involved in investment in India needs to be more vigilant. This means the institutional investors, the stockbrokers, the small investors, suppliers, customers, the financial press and employees. Too many easy deals are done under the table and winked at by those who should be more alert. Until recently there was a feeling that reputed big business tycoons could be trusted—they had built companies, become well known, had wide influence and were widely quoted in the media. Well, my experience has shown that you can trust them like you can trust a python! Can you imagine so-called reputed business families selling their own shares on the stock market while not intending to transfer these shares to the new owners? If this is not fraud, what is?

Management Forum, Calcutta
3 January 1986

Democracy and Economic Reforms

This is the eleventh national poll in India. It is also the largest democratic election ever held in human history, involving 590 million people over a distance greater than that from Scandinavia to Spain. This particular election comes at a time when many of the fundamental ideas which shaped modern India, and which endured for decades, are subject to challenge and change. Some, such as democracy, will remain. Some, such as a planned economy, will give way. But, the overall thrust of reform cannot now be rolled back. The actual benefits of these policies have not gone much beyond the wealthier and middle classes. Yet, the underprivileged understand that more reforms mean a better chance for them. In what other way can their lives be substantially improved in a relatively short period of time? The incredible expansion of the electronic media in India—itself a consequence of reform—has provided the poorest with the visuals of a better life. They are beginning to accept that there is only one way to get it.

Confederation of British Industry
29 April 1996

Non-Resident/Overseas Indians (NRI)

The NRI journey has just begun. As we build the community abroad, we create a new dimension of India. And if it works, as it appears to be doing, it will be one of the most extraordinary cultural achievements in human history. In a way, the destiny of the Indian ethos is in NRI hands. This is what should inspire us as we make our lives in the homes of our choice. It is a call truly in keeping with the finest ideals of the ancient rishis who proclaimed Vasudaiva Kutumbakam—the world is a unified entity and we all belong to it.

Non-Resident Indians Convention, Delhi
20 December 1995

In the contemporary political, social and economic contexts the Indian communities can make a great contribution. In years past, the NRIs have been occasionally politically active, but they have not always obtained a position equal to their importance. At this moment, when violence is breaking out all over, we are the inheritors of the Gandhian legacy. It is increasingly clear that only the path of non-violence will bring the kind of peace for which societies yearn. The message of Gandhiji can work, and I hope that NRIs all over the world will see this as a contribution they can make to the countries in which they live.

The ethics of non-violence is timely in a situation where ideologies of left and right are proving bankrupt. This is as true in India as it is in the world at large.

Non-Resident Indians Convention, Delhi
20 December 1995

Years ago, Rabindranath Tagore said: 'India is destined to be the teacher of all lands.' Sri Aurobindo echoed the same sentiments when he wrote that Mother India is not simply a piece of earth, she is a power that will lead. At that time, they had no idea of an expatriate Indian community of the size we now have. Looking at things, I do not know whether India itself will teach all lands. However, the fulfilment of these sage prophecies may well be in the NRI population which has a unique opportunity to contribute to the world today.

Global Organization of People of
Indian Origin Conference (GOPIO), New York
2 June 1995

There are ancient cultures which live no more. There are living and vigorous cultures which are not ancient. We are fortunate in having a heritage that is both old and vibrant. Indeed, the NRI segment of Indian life is its most dynamic expression. Some talk of 5,000 years of history and civilization. What is it worth if we cannot demonstrate that such history and civilization has the strength to compete in the modern world? But if we can show the world, through our achievements in other countries, that we have a message and a method, we have done a splendid service to India. A message in its homeland is good. A message with practical evidence of its success outside its homeland is great.

Non-Resident Indians Seminar, New Jersey
30 May 1995

NRIs are concerned about a recurrent theme—the image of corruption. NRIs are too close to India to be bluffed. They live and work in societies where corruption may exist, but it is not rewarded and is often heavily punished. Can we say the same about India today? Or have we reached a condition where the widespread toleration of public corruption has become an accepted feature of our life? The general NRI view is that every act of corruption reduces their investment. How difficult it is to cope with this if you live abroad and your money is here in India.

Non-Resident Indians Convention, Delhi
20 December 1995

Very soon—in the next ten years—NRIs will have to face a major social issue. Within our community the cultural orientation of our youth is changing. India is in danger of losing the next generation of NRIs. If India values NRIs it has to become more attractive to NRI youth. NRI youth will be much less patient than our generation with foibles and obstructions.

Non-Resident Indians Seminar, New Jersey
30 May 1995

The estimates differ widely, but there are now more than 15 million people of Indian origin who live outside India. Collectively, this is about the population of Australia or Sri Lanka. It is five times larger than Singapore and a little less than the population of Taiwan. If NRIs were a country on their own, our gross economic product would probably put us within the top twenty economies in the world. In short, the total economic output of Indians outside India is not much less than the gross national product of 900 million Indians who live in India. Such a community deserves the best community organizations in the world. All of us NRIs must work to see that we get such organizations.

GOPIO Conference, New York
2 June 1995

NRIs can say one thing with great pride—Indian communities around the world have generally been among the least violent of minority groups. Yet, given our conduct and our relative importance, we could play a much greater role in the public life of the countries in which we live. Gandhiji's message was not passive involvement but active participation. This requires both a change of attitude and much more effective community mobilization.

GOPIO Conference, New York
2 June 1995

The relationship between the NRI community and India needs to be much more precisely defined. Are we children or stepchildren of our motherland? Are we only courted when India is in economic trouble or financial distress? Successive governments have made promises to NRIs which still await fulfilment. NRIs all over the world are anxious to participate in the development of India and await the call. But each participation must be fair and fully recognized and not given second-class status.

Non-Resident Indians Conference, Washington, D.C.
10 May 1985

Appendix II

A PHILOSOPHY OF LIFE

In life, we not only have our successes. It is the very nature of life itself to have disappointment, and to make mistakes. On the eve of our Independence, Gandhiji said: 'Freedom is not worth having if it does not include the freedom to make mistakes.' This is the price we pay for adulthood—for growing up and becoming independent. We will, at times, be hurt, be disappointed, be frustrated, be angry. Every race cannot always be won. To face the disappointments that are inevitable in life, it is necessary to have discipline. Without discipline, life can be a very painful experience: with discipline, we can make the most of life by coping with the troubles and taking the successes with maturity.

Apeejay Schools Prize Convocation, Delhi
28 December 1990

Those of us who have been fortunate enough to live long in our world realize that most things are fleeting—money comes and goes, love is subject to emotional upheavals, power passes. One of the very few enduring things is true friendship.

Michael Foot Felicitation, London
19 November 1992

One must also look at life in proportion. Material development is not full development. Wealth can make a better life, but will it make a better person? Whilst this is a difficult question for people like me—people who, as businessmen, make a living by the creation of wealth—it is a fundamental question for our modern consumer society. The Hindu tradition, from which I come, looks at this problem in a more transcendent way. It constantly reminds us of the impermanence of phenomena and that the ultimate reality is the mystical merger of the individual soul with the Absolute—the great soul of the universe.

International Development Forum, New York
1 June 1995

I believe that absolute equality of opportunity, removal of discrimination between men and women, is a fundamental necessity. Only when this happens will other divisions begin to disappear. If the system discriminates against women—that is about one-half of our population—it will discriminate against other groups which are smaller in size. So, this is where any society with commitment must start. Such an effort will also help society to see that we must focus our economic and political policies on the whole of society and not on any particular or favoured part of society.

Lions Club, Calcutta
29 December 1988

To many people, education means studies and learning from teachers and textbooks. This is only one segment of education. The true purpose of education is to build character—to develop that quality of personality that gives us moral strength. Many of you may ask: 'What is character?' It is difficult to give a very clear definition, but it is something that strengthens your moral determination. Character is what makes you stand firm and carry on when you know that you are right—even if everyone is against you. Character is what gives you a sense of justice and fair play. Character is what gives us the strength to carry out our principles, admit our mistakes, and to face life with confidence in ourselves and what we believe in.

Apeejay Schools Prize Convocation, Delhi
28 December 1990

Children are the greatest asset, and also the weakest segment, in any society. Their pain is our pain. Their distress is the distress of civilization. If we neglect the children of the world, we neglect the future of the world. Our attitude to the problems of children tells us a great deal about ourselves.

National Society for the Prevention of
Cruelty to Children, London
2 November 1995

In less than five years, there comes a day which comes only once in a thousand years. On January 1st in the year 2000 we will celebrate a new year, a new century and a new millennium. The youth generation speaks to and speaks for that time. As you do, I ask you to recall two tested truths. First, never forget a warning from distant mythology: Hubris is inevitably followed by Nemesis. Second, remember that the verities of the past may take new guises, but many perennial questions remain. With Eve and Oedipus, we still wonder: where are the limits of human knowledge? With Job and Electra, we still ask: why do the good suffer? With Joan of Arc and Hamlet, we still puzzle: how do the innocent confront evil? With Cleopatra and Willy Loman, we still reflect: what is fate?

Chapman University, California
26 May 1996

Leadership is the obligation which academic achievement owes to education. When educated men and women shirk the roles of leadership, society pays a terrible price because public life becomes the domain of the less knowledgeable.

Chapman University, California
26 May 1996

Wealth: Ethics and Obligations

I am, as you know, a businessman. In order to conduct business affairs in a responsible way, one needs to adhere to certain basic values—belief in hard work, in competition, in innovation and in enterprise. When all these come together you will generally find that the businessman is successful. But there is something more important than success—and that is a sense of ethics. Too many businessmen feel that material success is an end in itself. If life could be evaluated in monetary terms, this attitude would be acceptable. However, many of us believe that we have, ultimately, to face a higher judgement than ourselves and that belief instils in us a moral code. Even the less spiritually oriented among us cannot forget that they belong to the extended system. Wherever we live, we remain essentially a family oriented community. In such an environment, your children and all your relations are important. Ultimately, it is only your own sense of ethics which will evoke their respect and bind the family together. A businessman without ethics may be financially successful, but will be without honour in his own home. But ethics is not only morality and correct behaviour in one's profession and one's home; that is a narrow view. Ethics involves responsibility and responsibility relates not only to the family, but also involves service to others.

Indian Society of West Wales
23 January 1987

Hinduism addresses the question of wealth through its emphasis on duty. The life of each individual is ideally ordered into different stages. During the stage of worldly participation—the stage known as the householder period—it is the duty of a person to undertake material tasks for the sake of the family and society. As age comes, detachment is another duty. Finally, renunciation is the task of old age. What Hinduism teaches us is that the pursuit of wealth may be permissible, but attachment to it is not. My own personal experience suggests that wealth is the reward for personal effort. However, it is not everything. I came to this country many years ago because of a personal family tragedy—and all the money in the world could not prevent that tragedy which illness brought. There is, to me, an intellectual challenge in the creation of wealth, but there are limitations to the value of wealth.

St James's Rectory, Piccadilly, London
4 November 1985

One of the paradoxes of life is that the responsibilities of wealth are most difficult to accept. Yet they are most needed. This is where self-restraint becomes so important. We must all remember that wealth is often a most dangerous substance. It imparts arrogance, and arrogance combined with the power of wealth can become a social menace. So how can we encourage self-restraint in those who would misuse wealth to obtain various kinds of power? I believe the answer lies in moral values. To be really effective, restraint must come from within the individual—

restraint which stems from a sense of responsibility and thus produces moral concerns. Unfortunately, restraint is not born in us. It must be taught by example. This is where responsibility has an extended function that reaches into all walks of life. Those who accept the need for moral values must not only practice but, to some extent, also preach. I do not mean evangelize—I mean discuss and make known the principles by which one lives. We, and I mean all of us, must also apply principles to our wealth. The obligations of wealth are costly, but the cost of not accepting those obligations eventually is much higher.

Indian Welfare Society, London
14 March 1992

I believe in the free enterprise system because I think it does three things: it encourages the individual, it is efficient, and it creates wealth at a rapid rate. For the free enterprise system to work does not require much intervention. But for the free enterprise system to work well requires constant vigilance. This is where responsibility is linked to wealth. A system which encourages the creation of wealth without corresponding responsibilities is like a car in motion without a driver—the momentum is there but it is a public danger. If human nature were perfect, wealth would have an automatic and inbuilt set of responsibilities. Because human nature is not perfect, society has to structure appropriate obligations.

St James's Rectory, Piccadilly, London
4 November 1985

It is only saints who speak of renunciation. Most other people, including economists and analysts of society, agree that wealth, and its continued creation, is essential for everybody. It is the foundation for material development and the key to the conventional vision of a better life.

Disagreements arise over the circumstances in which wealth is created and how it is to be distributed. But, of the need to produce wealth there is no dispute. Wealth is also relative, and a matter of perception. There are many people who are looked upon as being extremely wealthy—some people think I am one of them—but who are, in effect, not rich at all. It is attitude that shapes our relationship to wealth. Some believe that wealth is a trust. Money that is generated is constantly reinvested. This reinvestment is what benefits society. My own view is different. I believe that wealth is like a tranquillizer—sometimes it is helpful to the system, especially when properly administered. However, one must not become dependent on it, nor enslaved by it. One must always be prepared to do without it, and not be too affected by the loss.

Indian Welfare Society, London
14 March 1992

We need both responsibilities and obligations. The very fact that we are human imposes obligations on us. The more assets we have, the more our obligations should be. This is a moral necessity. It is also a practical protection. Wealth without responsibility, the attitude of the greedy in a needy world, provokes the reaction that causes the loss of wealth. Modern political revolutions underline this truth.

St James's Rectory, Piccadilly, London
4 November 1985

In general, and at our time in history in particular, it is correct to say that knowledge, without an ethical base, is a loose cannon—dangerous to all and most dangerous to those who have knowledge of, or manage, money. The human species is rapidly approaching the moment at which our great leaps in knowledge will destroy us, unless we temper it with wisdom. This is as true in business as it is in all human affairs. The recent crop of business shake-ups—in America, in this country, even in India—are due to ethical misjudgements, not to bad financial or marketing decisions. Some of the most talented members of the business community have fallen victim in these situations. It is increasingly clear that good ethics is good business, that good ethics is good entrepreneurship and good management.

Cranfield School of Management, UK
6 May 1987

History

The great thinkers of history will tell us that the best way in which to understand the future is by examining the past. The lessons of history are guides for tomorrow. If we know what others have experienced, if we appreciate what past events have taught the human species, we can perhaps avoid some of the dreadful mistakes that our ancestors made. George Santayana, the great European philosopher, once said: 'To be ignorant of history is to be condemned to repeat its mistakes.' How are we to learn from history? There are many ways of doing this—there is the history of events, there is the history of ideas, there is the history of social groups, and many other histories. And then, there is another kind of history—the history of history makers. In this sense, history speaks to us through the lives of great men and women—leaders who illuminate the record of human experience.

Harrow School, UK
26 May 1986

We live at a moment in human history when we need all our resources of mind and spirit. Great technological developments have taken place, but in the service of what ends are they to be used? Great political changes have transformed the global agenda. Yet, we are still questing for systems and structures that can assure peace and freedom from fear. Great economic progress has created spectacular engines of wealth creation. Now, for the first time ever, we live in an international market and a planetary economy. However, economic insecurity has increased and large numbers of people feel left behind. The achievements have been outstanding but, unless we correct their focus and moderate their distortions, our successes will recoil on themselves and become endangered.

Chapman University, California
26 May 1996

Ours is a moment of social transition. The values which once animated societies are changing rapidly. Large numbers of people, young and old, are unsure of who they are and what they want in life. Almost every part of the world is more modern, but much less emotionally secure. The special victim of contemporary society is the family, and all that the family stands for.

Non-Resident Indians Convention, Delhi
20 December 1995

Among the great dangers we face today are the dangers of overspecialization. Thirty years ago the great Spanish philosopher, José Ortega y Gasset, warned the Western world of a new barbarism. The new barbarians, he said, would be the specialized technologists, scientists and professionals who would strive for straight-line excellence without regard to the human and environmental consequences of their pursuits. George Orwell, in his book *1984*, reinforced those sentiments. Perhaps our failure to heed the cries of Ortega and Orwell produced the brutality of Bhopal, the tragedy of Challenger and the calamity of Chernobyl. All these are warnings that contain a poignant message for all peoples today: specialization may be necessary, but a broad cultural and humanistic perspective is essential.

American College of Switzerland, Leysin
10 May 1986

The Global World Today

Modern society demands of us that we be both international and national-minded at one and the same time. Today, it is virtually impossible to be successful in any major field of endeavour unless one has an understanding of the international dimensions of one's activities. In public life, in business, in the professions, in research, in most areas, the boundaries between what is national and what is international are fast disappearing.

London School of Economics
11 March 1987

We are now living in a seriously divided world. Those divisions reach down from the level of international affairs to the home and the family. In many countries, including our own, the persistence of these divisions will create various kinds of civil wars and other conflicts. If these escalate, what is the use of all the reforms and liberalizations in the world? This is not an Indian disease, it is not an Eastern or Western, Northern or Southern sickness. It is a global problem. As you know, I live in England, but my business requires that I spend much time in Europe, America and elsewhere.

It is the same story everywhere—societies, communities, families and homes are deeply divided. This is the real threat to all countries and to international and local order.

Rotary Club of Calcutta
27 December 1994

For those of us who are interested in world affairs, this is a striking moment in world history. Rarely, if ever before, have so many historic changes taken place simultaneously. These are fundamental movements whose real meaning will only be clarified in time. Perhaps we need the Chinese appreciation of time; when Mao Zedong was asked about the importance of the French Revolution, he replied: 'It is too early to tell!' Somewhere, between the urgent and the immediate, are the deeper historical events that alter the shape of the world. Among them today are the efforts of three major nations to restructure their ways of life. Russia, China and India together count for nearly one-half of the world's population. And this half of the world is trying to create something new—by embarking on policies and priorities that are utterly different from the past. They are rejecting the very concepts that have been at the heart of the development of their societies. These are the real revolutions—the real revelations of our time.

World Affairs Council, Orange County, California
13 October 1992

Currently, we are living at the crossroads of three great transitions. A major political transition has come with the end of the Cold War. Old ideologies have gone, many new countries have emerged and other states are trying to find their place in the new universe around us. The danger of a world war has receded, but vicious violence is worse than ever. And now the victims are increasingly civilians and non-combatants, including children. We also live in a time of social transition. The values which once animated societies are changing rapidly. Large numbers of people, old and young, are unsure of who they are and what they want in life. Almost every part of the world is more modern, but much less emotionally secure. The special victim of contemporary society is the family, and all that the family stands for. At the same time, some kind of a major economic transformation is taking place. There is a much greater appreciation of the contribution of free enterprise in every part of the world. I do not know whether this is a capitalist revolution or not. But, everywhere, governments which distrusted the market are now accepting market forces as engines of the economy. I was recently in South Africa. It is remarkable how the African National Congress, a long and sincere proponent of state involvement in the economy, has converted to free enterprise. In many areas of Asia and Africa, the socialized bureaucracy was once the most powerful element in the government. Now, it is seen as the principal enemy of growth, progress and prosperity.

GOPIO Conference, New York
2 June 1995

Today, it is virtually impossible to be successful in any major field of endeavour unless one has an understanding of the international dimensions of one's activities. In public life, in business, in the professions, in research, in most areas the boundaries between what is international are fast disappearing. All of us are citizens of the world in a way which our forebears never were. Now, we have to expand the dimensions of our thinking to accept these horizons for which our traditions have not prepared us. If we accept them and integrate them into our visions, we will make great gains—individual and societal.

American College of Switzerland, Leysin
10 May 1996

The spirit of internationalism, the openness to multicultural experiences, and the appreciation of human dignity are themes that are essential in today's world. We have to be both international and national-minded at one and the same time. Never before in history have these qualities, generally contradictory ones, been required to blend in the degree that they are now required. And the crucible of the mix is the human personality—the most difficult of all melting vessels.

American College of Switzerland, Leysin
10 May 1996

Appendix III

BUSINESS AND ECONOMICS

The New Global Economy

Ours is a particularly challenging time in economic history. There are now virtually no barriers to the free flow of ideas and capital across national borders. Most goods which are in demand also somehow find their way into markets that want them. This is a major change from just a few years ago. Yet, these changes have provoked certain reactions. International economics is congealing into powerful concentrations, formal or informal trading blocs such as those in Western Europe, North America or the East Pacific. Countries and economies in-between, nations such as India, now have to become exceptionally competitive if they are to be successful in this new world. Thus, the reforms in India are hardly a matter of choice. They are a matter of necessity and they have not come a day too soon. Without the reforms of the past two years,

India would have been consigned to the lower ranks of global economies for decades to come.

World Marketing and Management Congress, Delhi
4 January 1994

In recent years there have been remarkable changes in the international political economy. Perhaps the best way to describe these changes is to say that we have moved from a world of superpowers to a world of super markets. Large markets that once were closed have begun to open. Some have been fruitful and others disappointing. Nonetheless, the main factor which drives the global economy today is the principle of liberalized markets.

SMI Conference, London
31 January 1996

In the past five years or so there has been unusual and almost complete acceptance of capitalism as the organizing principle of economies all over the world. The experiments with state socialism are over. Even the mixed economies are shedding their state-owned enterprises. It is now clear that most people in the West and elsewhere believe that government should not, and cannot, effectively own and manage economic enterprises. This, of course, has opened the doors to the two major elements of capitalism—the business entrepreneur, corporate or otherwise, and the market itself. As economic transactions are increasingly conducted on a business, or a business-to-business basis, they may be more efficient and they certainly are more competitive in the West.

Delhi University
21 December 1994

There is another lesson we can note from the Asia-Pacific area. Countries which open their economies to the world have prospered far beyond those who cherish a more protected economic environment. There is often a cultural price to pay for such modernization. But, in the long run, a culture cannot isolate itself in today's global environment. Surely, a cultural tradition is preserved more by the morals and ethics of individuals and families than by building cultural and economic walls which impoverish people. A closed economy is now a poor economy.

Institute of Marketing and Management, Delhi
5 January 1996

Business: Philosophy and Reflections

There are really no mystical secrets to success in business, at home or abroad. The foundation is hard work and an intimate knowledge of what you do. Then, when opportunities come, as they often do in the business world, you will be ready for them. It is truly said that genius is 90 per cent perspiration and 10 per cent inspiration.

Cranfield School of Management, UK
6 May 1987

People grow old, they get stale, they get overcautious, and they do not always learn the appropriate lessons from experience. Add to this the fact that, sometimes, the managers who are good for boom times are not necessarily the same as those who are good for recession. I have seen near miracles performed in old established companies, simply by changing the managing director to someone from outside the industry. Someone who is prepared to look stupid by asking why do we make it this way, and why do we put up with this customer practice; someone who can find new answers and ideas without being weighed down by the baggage of years of experience. Please don't get me wrong—experience counts—but so does the ability to invent new experiences.

Alumni Association, Indian Institutes of Technology,
Cambridge, Massachusetts
21 April 1994

Never sit back on a successful idea. Always have alternate strategies in mind and think ahead of how to implement them. Nobody has a permanent monopoly on any idea, however effective it may be.

Financial Times World Steel Conference, London
21 March 1996

A caution about fashion—don't blindly follow the crowd and chase after a mirage. I firmly believe you have to have a degree of counter cyclical thinking. There is no point in moving into a business sector when everyone else is rushing in, and its potential has been fully recognized. Look, for example, at the billions of dollars lost by our highly respected institutions and banks as they rushed into real estate and stockbroking at the top of the market. If you go with the crowd you'll find costs of entry will be high and overcapacity will be reached sooner. Popularity does not guarantee success.

Massachusetts Institute of Technology
30 April 1993

Never sacrifice your enthusiasm or vision to other people's constraints. I am often asked by young people to suggest a product or industry they go into. I usually refuse, explaining that: 'Wisdom and sagacity are things one only gets with age, so their application has drawbacks.' In other words, do not let my old man's wisdom restrict your youthful horizons! The vigour and freshness of youth is a great resource which we sometimes undervalue. There are always new ways of looking at things. Do not be afraid to ask 'why?' Often, those not weighed down with the baggage of years can find new answers. But first, they must find the confidence to ask.

Oxford University
9 June 1993

One of the dangers in any kind of business is that the most obvious path appears the easiest. This is misleading because it often involves costs that are higher than they initially appear to be. Sometimes a more innovative approach may take longer and look more expensive, but is far more productive in the long run. Experts will not tell you this. It is tempting, then, to say: Do not listen to the experts. But that is too extreme. What I would say is: Listen carefully but make your own judgements. Often, this kind of judgement has to be made not only on an examination of what is, but also on faith in what might be. Imagination does play a role in evaluation.

Financial Times World Steel Conference, London
21 March 1996

At every stage of business activity there are lessons to be learned, sometimes painfully and sometimes at considerable cost. The learning process continues because every phase presents different challenges. Each experience presents us with new perspectives. It seems to me that the most basic lesson of all is this: when you stop learning, it's time to stop doing business.

Financial Times World Steel Conference, London
21 March 1996

Caparo is something more than just a business. We have been guided and supported by two ideological pledges. The first—our conviction that while all business is local, business-building today requires a global vision. The second—our belief that industrial manufacturing is a worthy activity with a prosperous potential. There is a common misperception that industrial manufacturing businesses are pedestrian. My entire career has been committed to challenging the logic of this pessimism. Effective management and the innovative use of human and technical resources does make industrial manufacturing both exciting and rewarding.

Society of Manufacturing Engineers, Baltimore
3 June 1995

The definition of opportunity is changing—changing towards excellence. It is the quality of markets, the quality of labour and the longer term stability of profits which are today's measurement of opportunity. Superiority of the infrastructure, the nature of work culture, the level of individual productivity, the competence of local managers, the global geographic position—these are the modern components of opportunity.

Bengal Initiative, Calcutta
29 December 1995

I am an avid seeker of growth and I explain it as follows: the human condition seeks to better itself whether materially or intellectually. And the most exciting period of life is one's teens and early twenties. During those years, tremendous things are happening physiologically. If you can somehow capture that excitement and freshness in an organization, you've got something. That's what I mean by growth. It isn't acquisitiveness or size. It's the vivacity it gives to life in the company. Recognize those exciting feelings while you are still young and try to instil them throughout the whole of your working life.

Massachusetts Institute of Technology
30 April 1993

Management Methods and Approaches

Thinking about my own career, I encourage all of you to do two things. First, never neglect the opportunity to get some first-hand experience of the working conditions of the lowest paid production worker in your business. Go to the workshop, to the factory, to the clerical desk. Talk to production workers, clerks and minor employees. You can learn much more from them than from those who sit in air-conditioned offices and communicate only by memo or telephone. Judge a business not by the way the higher paid executives talk, but by how the lower paid employees feel. Second, try to get some international exposure or experience. The world of business is fast becoming one market place. We also have to learn to do business with a multiplicity of business cultures—socialist, communist, free enterprise, mixed enterprise and the like. Whatever our personal values may be, there is no room for insularity in business any more. If you have chances for working abroad, travelling abroad or studying abroad—take them. These are the building blocks of your future. No successful entrepreneur of the next generation will be able to function without some international experience—the spirit of enterprise now transcends cultural barriers.

Management Institute, Haryana
19 December 1987

Don't frustrate your managers by endorsing luxury perks for the big bosses. Make them feel that their entrepreneurial skills will pay off for the whole company and for them personally—not for a few top executives alone.

Cranfield School of Management, UK
6 May 1987

The ability to think is not the prerogative of management alone. To me, real leadership is the encouragement of communications up and down and the inclusion of inputs by others in decision making.

International Management Institute, Delhi
5 January 1996

A large part of the productivity problem comes from the impersonal nature of most modern enterprises—enterprises which treat workers as things, not as individual persons. I have always tried to make my employees feel that they are part of a family. At first, I was told by many productivity experts that this was an outdated and old-fashioned way of operating. However, I have found that workers respond very well to this approach. It makes them feel that there is a human and personal bond which is often lacking in modern society. In many ways I have found this approach useful in dealing with the unions too. The nature of modern production, and its complexity, makes effective coordination an essential element in business success. The teamwork concept, applied at all levels, is now a key ingredient in coordinating management efforts and improving management–worker relations. My experience suggests that a familial approach is much more rewarding than the finest organizational chart!

Sheffield Management Research Group, UK
4 February 1988

Try not to make long-term planning your sole master, and to be responsive to opportunities that may arise which you might never have envisaged. Opportunities, like beauty, lie in the eye of the beholder and, like luck, have to be worked for—they don't just drop from heaven. We must never overlook the importance of luck, although we must understand what luck is. To me, luck is one of the three words in my business lexicon—the other two are 'profit' and 'cash flow'. But, luck is not just chance, it is an opportunity waiting to happen. The only way you can have luck is to be prepared so that, when an opportunity presents itself, you can take advantage of it. People may call you 'lucky' but you will know better.

Sheffield Management Research Group, UK
4 February 1988

An important Caparo management theme concerns equipment. We always begin with the best facilities we can afford and aim for the highest possible productivity. There are some who believe that one can economize on machinery; that the trade-off between cost and efficiency justifies less expensive but less modern equipment. To my mind, this is very short-sighted. I would rather abandon a project than compromise on the quality of production. Remember that what is merely satisfactory is the enemy of what is best. Caparo has an overriding goal regarding labour: make the workforce as flexible as possible with no old-fashioned demarcations of activity. If you visit any of our plants you will see a blur between production people, fitters, maintenance and others. Everyone is prepared to do any job they are capable of doing. Production techniques have benefited enormously from the systems approach. The same notion should be applied to production personnel.

International Management Institute, Delhi
5 January 1996

My experience suggests that people are the key element, and a large proportion of my time is spent on talent management. In the past decade or two, there has been a fundamental shift in the loyalties and priorities of managers and workers. Once upon a time, employees' commitments were to the businesses they worked for. More recently, for a variety of social and political reasons, their loyalties have focused on themselves. One of our tasks, if we are to build successful enterprises, is to recover some of that loyalty and commitment to the firm. Unless we can do this, enterprise will become so individualized that it will flourish at the expense of companies.

Cambridge University/India Society
25 November 1989

We had, and still have, no predetermined strategy, other than the strategy of opportunity. And opportunity we define as any situation where new thinking and new management approaches can realize our basic criteria. We are always ready to examine any situation, to make speedy decisions on investment, and to commit our resources wherever opportunity matches our skills. We take well-thought-out risks, but please do not mistake this risk-taking for recklessness.

Cambridge University/India Society
25 November 1989

Things do not always go according to plan. Whether starting a new plant or taking over an existing company, make sure that you have more than enough financial resources to cope with the unexpected: machines do not always arrive on time, customers often take longer to place orders than forecast, and always take longer to pay. Any of these things can throw you badly off course, with the result that you lose control of your project. So, if you want to stay in control—and which manager worthy of the name does not—make sure that the downside risk is also included in your financial planning.

Alumni Association, Indian Institutes of Technology,
Cambridge, Massachussetts
21 April 1994

Managers must learn to market before they sell. This requires a long-term approach and a business-building perspective. Try and concentrate effort—too many exporters chase after numbers of little orders when they should be persistently focusing on a few big customers Don't be seduced into using cheap technology for production—the best technology is always really the cheapest in the long run. And, above all, do not be led into the quick fix, hit-and-run, fast buck attitude. This is a gambling strategy and, like some casino tactics, it works occasionally. But, if you seek a continuing and consistent business, there is no substitute for persistent and steady cultivation of profitable markets.

Delhi University
21 December 1994

In industrial relations, the way to deal with disputes is not to try to browbeat people into a docile state of mind. It is to identify a community of interest. This is why the key words in modern industrial relations are 'empowerment', 'involvement' and 'commitment'. We should be looking at how to get rid of the need to strike, not the right to strike. That can only be done by building relationships at work based on partnership and trust. People expect to be treated fairly and to have a say over matters that concern them at work. Good management is about fostering cooperation, not confrontation. If there is a feeling of fairness and unity of purpose within the company, everybody wants to work.

House of Lords, London
22 January 1997

Entrepreneurship

The term 'entrepreneur' has become closely associated with business enterprise, and with the creative instinct which is so much a part of successful business and professional endeavours. To my way of thinking, success in business, and other professions, is not only making profits. It is building: building capital, building an organization, building markets, building skills. To build in a lasting way, one has to be like an architect—a plan has to be developed, resources have to be assembled, plan approvals have to be obtained, construction strategies have to be evolved, and one has to have a clear idea of the final goal. In order to accomplish this, management alone is not enough. It is necessary to have a kind of creative insight—that is entrepreneurship.

Rotary Club of Calcutta
2 January 1984

I am often asked how to define an entrepreneur. My answer is anyone who has these five qualities: first, motivation beyond monetary incentives; second, the ability to do work one doesn't like as effectively as work that one does; third, needs little sleep and takes few holidays; fourth, never worries about a pension; fifth, is not afraid to lower one's standard of living.

Management Institute, Haryana
5 January 1996

It is not easy to find the skills of the entrepreneur—the skills of risk-taking, challenge and innovative style—combined with those of the manager. But unless they combine effectively there is little place for them separately in modern business. While natural talent is a powerful asset, I am also convinced that these skills can be taught and learned. This is why I urge you to supplement your training in business studies with broad educational inputs. In my personal decision making, some of the insights I have gained from the humanities and the social sciences have helped me even more than the business disciplines I have learned. It is this broad perspective that makes the manager an entrepreneur and the entrepreneur a manager!

Management Institute, Haryana
19 December 1987

There are many who say that enterprise—i.e., the ability to energize, mobilize and activate a business organization—is a talent with which one is born. It is true that the great entrepreneurs—the most dazzling exponents of the calculated risk—may have a certain natural genius which attends their efforts. However, I believe that enterprise can be learned, can be communicated and can be injected into a business.

Indo-US Chamber of Commerce, New York
15 February 1989

Management needs not only administrative competence but also entrepreneurial skills. Effective management must be supported by a sense of enterprise—the ability to seize an opportunity and act with speed and clarity. Good managers not only know their own goals—they communicate them clearly and act on them fast. In fact, I will go so far as to say that no decision is often much worse than a bad decision in business.

Cranfield School of Management, UK
6 May 1987

The task of the entrepreneur is to enhance his capital. He often seeks to do this through investment, appreciation and growth. In this process, we sometimes forget a basic fact of business life: bad management destroys capital in a rapid, and frequently imperceptible, way. Watch how your managers manage their capital if you want to preserve what you have. This is one of the key elements I use in evaluating those who work with me.

Cranfield School of Management, UK
6 May 1987

At times, business is a hard and testing field. In today's world, the businessman has to deal with so many influences outside the area of business itself and outside the purviews of his direct control. Yet, in this very broadening of our range of activity comes an interesting new challenge: we businessmen are probably closer to the pulsebeat of society than many other professionals. That is why our rewards are all the greater!

Management Institute, Haryana
19 December 1987

Business in Britain

Those who do business in more lax or permissive societies tend to think that the culture of special benefits due to position, high contacts, favours and inducements can be transplanted elsewhere. Sometimes, this appears to work for a while. In general, however, British business culture has no place for special benefits. Those who obtain them often have to pay heavily afterwards. Many countries, including India, can learn from the way in which Britain tries to reduce the impact of politics on business. The depoliticization of this sensitive nexus, the politics–business axis, allows businessmen of all ideologies to live and let live. The animosities which a culture of special benefits creates are thus much less evident in a society like Britain.

Nehru Centre, London
21 March 1994

If you have strong and sincere convictions, and are prepared to back them up with hard work and integrity, the conditions for success in Britain are good. My personal experience reinforces this conviction. When I began business here, I had few contacts and no track record. It was also a time when overseas businessmen were not as much encouraged as they are today. Yet, there were British suppliers, customers, and even banks who were prepared to accept our determination and our hard work as pledged assets. That same spirit prevails today in the sense that trust is defined by what you are, not by what you own.

Nehru Centre, London
21 March 1994

It used to be said that people who lived in Britain had hearts of oak. I don't know about that, but I can say that we must have spirits of steel to take the buffeting we have had in recent years. You will remember, and it is good to remember, that not long ago many analysts had written off our industry. The conventional wisdom held that our activities were rusty, antiquated and increasingly marginal. But, we have endured and the experience has given us confidence in the future. The facts are quite startling. About 70 per cent of steel products currently on the market have been developed only within the past ten years. The British steel industry produced an average of 80 tonnes of steel per employee in 1975. This year it is 421 tonnes—an increase of over 500 per cent in two decades. In 1994, our industry recorded the highest annual increase in productivity per employee: a 13 per cent gain over 1993. The energy consumed in our steel works has decreased by about 25 per cent since 1980. These are statistics of great pleasure for economists and number-crunchers. Only we know that they are statistics of great pain. But, they do show something of which we can be truly proud. For a long time, until very recently, the steel industry had a reputation for preferring tradition to innovation. We were generally considered to be conservative and slow to change. Yet, under the pressure of circumstance, we have responded with a speed and decisiveness that is a model for others. The moral is clear: we simply cannot do business in the same old way. It is change or perish—and how we have changed!

Lincolnshire Iron & Steel Institute, UK
7 April 1995

Britain is a country in which there are no short cuts to sustained success. Razzle-dazzle style, quick fixes and card-shuffling magic may have a short run of fortune, but those who stay the course are those who favour sound and level-headed approaches. This does not mean that entrepreneurship goes unrewarded. It only suggests that entrepreneurship must be underwritten with solid worth.

Nehru Centre, London
21 March 1994

The catalyst that joins a business together and energizes the whole is enterprise. It is this sense of venture and adventure, this activating enzyme, that produces the kind of excitement which makes an organization pulsate. If you look at the more successful British businesses you will see that this element has been basic to their success. As we enter the age of privatization we must learn to cultivate it, otherwise we shall simply be turning unenterprising nationalized operations into unenterprising corporate operations.

Sheffield Management Research Group, UK
4 February 1988

Sadly, during the 1960s and '70s, we had a history of industrial disputes in Britain which created a 'them and us' attitude. This was an important factor leading to our poor competitiveness. Industry today operates in an environment of intense competition. Trade unionists know that employer and employee are both subject to this pressure. Employees also need to know the aims and rules of a business in order to fully identify with it. Motivation and action requires clarity of purpose. This is what managers are struggling to achieve and if it is absent there is no point in penalizing the employees. An attack on the right to strike is a charter for the bad employer. In my opinion, good relationships between management and employees cannot be created by legislation.

House of Lords, London
22 January 1997

Index